Reading about revival cannc
time you are made aware of
will stimulate you to pray that he might once again come in revival blessing. Read Nigel Paterson's book with that expectation.

— **Terry Virgo**, Founder of Newfrontiers, Bible teacher and author of many books including *The tide is turning*

All great revivals begin or end in the home. Revival is about Jesus being in the midst, with nothing hindering. I have been encouraging Nigel Paterson for nearly ten years to write books, and this one is on the subject that he has most wanted to put into print. I hope that different denominations in the UK will make good use of this book.

— **Robert Hicks**, Christian publisher and author

Nigel Paterson has been a good friend and co-worker in the gospel for many years, both in the UK and abroad. He is a humble and prayerful servant of God, passionate about revival, and as such is well qualified to write about it. Not only is his research meticulous, he has chosen stories from the historical records that will inspire and challenge the reader to seek God for a heaven-sent move of revival power today. Our nation, and the whole world, needs this more than ever!

— **Martyn Dunsford MBE**, founder of Care and Relief for the Young (CRY) and pastor

I'm delighted that Nigel Paterson has written this single volume on the extensive subject of Christian revivals in the UK. If we don't need a revival now, then when? This book had to be written, and it has been done superbly.

— **Sir Anthony Seldon**, educator, author and contemporary historian, Vice-Chancellor of the University of Buckingham 2015-2020

A thought-provoking read. Nigel Paterson brings up some interesting facts that really got me thinking about revival in the UK. As a business person who specialises in change & career transition leadership, I think every Christian who is questioning in this season we are facing should read this book. It will help you understand why 'Change of the Tide' is coming and how to prepare for it.

— **Samuel T. Reddy**, Bestselling author of *Leavers To Leaders*, Advisor Impact Entrepreneur and Founder of TriAtis Global to Dominic De Souza

Change of the Tide

REVIVALS IN THE UK

Nigel Paterson

Nigel Paterson

RP | Regeneration Publications

First published autumn 2020

Published by Regeneration Publications, Southampton, United Kingdom

www.changeofthetide.com

ISBN 978-1-8382660-0-4

Acknowledgements
Scripture quotations are from the *New Living Translation* unless otherwise stated

A catalogue record of this book is available from the British Library

Text formatting by Donna Pendrey
Design and production arranged by Roger Chouler, Rochart
www.rochartportraits.com
Front cover design by Emma Kent
Cover photo of waves by Daniel Torobekov
Printed by Clays, Bungay, Suffolk, England

Contents

Foreword		7
Preface		9
Introduction		11
1.	The Reformation as a revival and its Puritan legacy	23
2.	The Evangelical Awakening beginning in 1727	44
3.	Aftermath of the Evangelical Awakening	66
4.	Later descendants of the Evangelical Awakening	88
5.	The 1859 Revival	108
6.	Aftermath of the 1859 Revival	129
7.	The Welsh Revival of 1904-1905 and beyond	148
8.	The rest of the twentieth century	172
9.	The twenty-first century and the coronavirus pandemic	197
10.	What should I be doing?	218
End Notes		228
Ongoing developments		239

Foreword

by Andy Johnston

I am a grandson of revival. In 1934 my grandmother, Gladys Boddy (a classic grandmother's name if ever there was one), wheeled my mother's pram into a tent "crusade" on Lister Drive, Tuebrook, Liverpool. The Pentecostal pioneer and healing evangelist Edward Jeffreys, son of Stephen and nephew of George Jeffreys, had come to town. On one day in June 1934 as many as 10,000 attended the meetings and 3,000 people responded to the Gospel, and this included my grandmother Gladys. Many others were healed as people got out of wheelchairs, saw their sight restored and their deaf ears unblocked. Revival came to the city of Liverpool in the dark days of the economic depression of the 1930s.

I came to Christ as a young boy, aged 11, in 1972 in a church which was planted as a result of the ministry of Edward Jeffreys. I can still remember listening in the Sunday evening communion services to the stories of the founding members of the Church, who had experienced the revival first hand. In particular, I remember Norman Moore. Norman must have been in his 80s by the time I knew him but, whenever he got up and spoke and testified of what he had seen God do in those revival days, his face would shine still, nearly 40 years on, with the glory of God and there would be tears of joy in his eyes. I will never forget the face of Norman Moore.

Since those days I have read much on the subject of revival. The stories of The Reformation and its Puritan legacy, of Whitfield and Wesley and the Methodist movement, of the 1859 revival in Northern Ireland, the 1904 Welsh revival, the Lewis outpouring in 1949 and many more have arrested my attention and caused me to pray the pray of the Old Testament prophet Habakkuk, "LORD, I have heard of your fame; I stand in awe of your deeds, O LORD. Renew them in our day, in our time make them known; in wrath remember mercy" (Habakkuk 3:1-2).

If you are anything like me, Nigel Paterson's concise study of revival will warm your heart. It is Church history at its best. God takes centre stage and displays His greatness and His glory. Good writers take complex stories and issues and makes them comprehensible and accessible for everyone who might be interested in the topic. Nigel does exactly this and, for this reason, I commend this book to you. My hope is that it will inspire you and, even more importantly, drive you to your knees in prayer.

Andy Johnston is Senior Pastor of King's Community Church (Southampton) and the author of *Convinced by scripture: The life of Martin Luther*

Preface

I was first introduced to the subject of revival by reading *Like a mighty wind* by Mel Tari. I had been born again into the Christian environment of Oxbridge in the early 1970s (having received invaluable input from friends at Oxford and Cambridge universities). It was a great environment for taking subjects like revival seriously. My knowledge of some of the characters and stories related in this book began then. It has got me reading much more, over the intervening decades, some of which is given in the End Notes.

Over ten years ago, I had recently had published online a Cambridge Paper, on the case for having one or more Christian universities in the United Kingdom. At a Christian event in London, I was asked by the Commissioning Editor of a well-known Christian publisher what I thought I might write next. I said I would like to write a book about how exactly God had broken into the country at key moments in its history.

As some readers will already know, that particular idea - structured around past revivals - is a massive one. Then, the 2020 first lockdown gave me the perfect opportunity to get the book written.

While writing, I have been deeply impressed by a sense of urgency about getting this book published before the end of 2020. If any readers would like to refer me to added, relevant sources of information on past revivals in the UK, I would be very interested to hear from them. I have many more references than I have cited, but that will not have stopped me missing some fine pieces of writing already out there. A contact email address can be found at changeofthetide.com

Nigel Paterson
October 2020

Introduction

This book is especially written so that a younger generation can learn about the many works of God in revival that have already happened in the United Kingdom. It is deliberately brief, and it does not assume a great deal of previous knowledge about past revivals or British history.

It is presented as much as possible as a narrative, where explanations are given as and when they seem essential to an understanding of the unfolding story featuring many people and places. It has been written with the positive view that these Christian revivals have been good for the country.

What is revival?

A *revival* is taken here to mean a *sovereign* (supreme) move of God upon a land, people, region, local community or even single individuals. It is an *outpouring* (= pouring out) of His Spirit and an outworking of His glory that defies full explanation in terms of human arrangements and capabilities. In revival, God has taken the field; He has laid bare His holy arm. Times of revival are typically, though not always, attended by occasions when some people are most visibly impacted: they fall to the ground, faint, lie motionless, cry out, laugh, keep repeating themselves or are convulsed. In fact, some people do one or more of these things when they are profoundly emotionally affected, so such behaviours are not exclusive to seasons of revival.

While no single phrase can hold all the characteristics of revival described above, a memorable and short definition given by Duncan Campbell was 'a people saturated with God'.

Revival leaves lasting impact on the church, individual believers, the formerly *unsaved* (people who were not Christians with a personal faith beforehand) and whole communities or societies, including some of the poorest and most in need. New *converts* (people turning to Christ) are so deeply affected by the experience that the large majority of them become lifelong followers of the Lord Jesus Christ. If all that does not happen, then maybe another good word is needed to describe the move of God that did happen. I find it helpful to distinguish between various levels of revival, which can be:

R1 R1 is full-on revival, where a whole nation (like Wales) or a group of nations are blanketed with God's activity. This book is mainly about such occasions.

R2 A region is impacted by revival.

R3 A community (town, city or large organisation) is impacted by revival.

R4 One or more individuals are so impacted that they typically seem to be like a walking revival. They may be capable of spreading revival wherever they go (e.g. Charles Finney, William and Catherine Booth, D.L. Moody).

The main revivals

The book is structured around the main countrywide (R1) revivals that have happened in the United Kingdom. These are: the Reformation, the Great Awakening of the eighteenth century, the Revival of 1859 and the Welsh Revival of 1904-1905 (which in fact spread to many other parts of the UK). Some revival scholars distinguish other main revivals in between, and the glorious things that did happen in those times are included here wherever known. As the narrative reaches the twentieth century and the time of living memory, there is more coverage given to the notable moves of God that have been less than national revivals.

The British Isles is a geographical name that broadly denotes the territory of the United Kingdom as it was before the Independence of the Republic of Eire in 1922. Great Britain is the geographical name of the main island of the United Kingdom, and is a name which is used more often by foreigners than by residents. Reference is given wherever possible to Great Britain's constituent three nations of England, Scotland and Wales. Northern Ireland is, of course, the other nation in the United Kingdom.

What revival is not

I suggest the following about full-on revival:

☑ It cannot be contained inside a single church or Christian organisation, as it is much greater than that. There has to be evidence of some subsequent strong impact on the local community as well. That is why this book takes an extensive interest in social impacts that sometimes took generations to work through.

- ☑ It should not be used to describe a move of God in successful evangelism where there was no spiritual life there beforehand. I suggest that is why there is no use of the word 'revive' in the New Testament, whereas there is plenty of its mention and need for it seen in the Old Testament. It is true that the churches written to in Revelation were in need of revival, but we do not know what prayers the church members prayed after receiving the apostle John's letter to them. It would have been very appropriate if some of their responding prayers began with 'Revive me…' and 'Revive us….'

- ☑ It cannot consist only in exciting records of conversion. Conversions, important as these are in this book, can be recorded in *evangelistic* events (about the good news of Jesus Christ) and campaigns that have proved later to have had little lasting impact in people's lives and communities.

- ☑ It is too holy a work of God to make fun of in some dark way. We need to treat the things of God with a holy fear (e.g. Uzziah in Old Testament days was judged for his irreverence in touching the ark of God against biblical instructions, 2 Samuel 6:6-7).

The concept of revival can also be confused with reformation, renewal, restoration and other memorable visitations of God. These other important works of God will be met in the course of the book.

Why past revivals matter

These major revivals were times that did the following:

1. They were significant breakthroughs for the Kingdom of God. It is part of the Lord's prayer to pray for God's kingdom to come (e.g. Luke11:2).
2. They involved thousands, if not millions, of people finding their way into a living relationship with Jesus Christ. A notable number of the new believers had been so steeped in sin or contrary thinking that many of them had been far beyond the reach of a local church.
3. They affected communities, households and individuals for the better. Communities have been so deeply affected in times of revival that it is very difficult to imagine how else an ungodly nation can be turned around again. The common morality of the nation is lifted. Violence, slavery and virtual slavery, other crimes, abuse, prostitution, drunkenness, drug-taking, divorce, ill-health and debt are all reduced. Marriage relationships, public health, the quality and quantity of work done, and the payment of long-standing debts are all affected positively. Politicians, business people and journalists are obliged to be more reliable. The nation assumes a higher sense of destiny.
4. They led to lasting social impacts, some of which have helped to shape and define the nation and its people.
5. They can serve as a key for understanding much of the Christian history of the country.

6. They point towards the primary place of God's sovereign working in and through real individuals, indicating how God has opened up the national culture in the past.

7. They show God's merciful character in bringing refreshing from His presence. 'And did those feet [of Jesus] walk upon England's green and pleasant land?' the hymn 'Jerusalem' by William Blake famously asks. There is a sense in which His feet have done just that many times (compare with Acts 1:1), though probably not in the way that Blake imagined.

8. They can encourage, inform and inspire Christians everywhere to long for revival in their own situations.[1]

Metaphors of revival

The metaphor implicit in the word 'revival' has had a relatively short history. This word, meaning 'a general religious awakening in a community', was first used at the beginning of the eighteenth century. It is a collective word for a practical occurrence that can be referred to using a number of other metaphors as well.

The Hebrew root word 'to live' is used almost three hundred times in the Old Testament. It means to bring to life, to cause to live, to enliven. The English language contains a very large vocabulary, so it is typical that one word in another language is translatable into several English ones, each with its own shade of meaning. Where the word 'enliven' means the giving of added life to people or situations that already have some life in them, the word 'revive' may be a suitable choice of word.

There are over 20 uses of the root Hebrew word that give some insight into revival. As part of that, the Psalmist of Psalm 119 prays 'Revive me…' nine times (NASB), encouraging the thought that the people of God need to pray for revival – first and foremost in themselves. Situations in need of revival are generally left to speak for themselves. *Revival* in general use means a bringing back of a full measure of life, a return of earlier vigour.

An awakening from sleep is another way of being revived. The contrast is made with being asleep and therefore inactive, unaware and unresponsive. There were times in Old Testament days when God called on His people to awake (Isaiah 51:17, 52:1). Their state of inaction was due to much more than sheer doziness. The genuine Christian life is that of a person whose eyes are open and whose faculties are alert and all functioning (Romans 13:11, Ephesians 5:14, 1 Thessalonians 5:6).

The awakening metaphor has the advantage that a clear, active response is needed to being awoken, which is to get up and get going. The sleepiness can be due to sorrow, despair or a sense of reeling from recent troubles and oppression. The wakefulness can be a new invigoration to serve God and others wholeheartedly, to be unashamed of Jesus Christ and to pray as though yours and other people's lives depend upon it.

A **Pentecost** sums up the sovereign move of God upon a people, like the unique events that occurred on the Day of Pentecost described in Acts 2. The word is used as another word for revival in a book title like *The Korean Pentecost and the sufferings which followed*, which describes the Korean revival of 1907 and the suffering that followed under foreign occupation.[2] Dr. Martyn Lloyd-Jones said that all revivals are in some way a return to Pentecost.[3]

A mighty wind is an expression used to describe a real sound that was heard by the followers of Jesus on the Day of Pentecost. On that day, all 'the believers were meeting together in one place. Suddenly, there was a sound from heaven like the roaring of a mighty windstorm, and it filled the house where they were sitting' (Acts 2:1-2). This metaphor is used in the title of *Like a mighty wind*, which tells the story of the revival on East Timor in 1965.[4]

Flames of fire followed the noise of a mighty wind on the Day of Pentecost: 'Then, what looked like flames or tongues of fire appeared and settled on each of them' (Acts 2:3). Those flames of fire were connected with the coming of the Holy Spirit to the disciples. As an example of use of the expression, The world on fire: *The Welsh revival and its lessons for our time* is the title of a recent book by Rick Joyner.[5]

Water is mentioned many times in the Bible, but one of its most important aspects is its symbolism of God's blessing and life-giving refreshment. God Himself is the fountain of living waters (e.g. Jeremiah 2:13). The flow of water can be used as a metaphor for the flow of the Holy Spirit (e.g. John 7:37-39). Water can come in the form of a shower of spring rain (Hosea 6:3), a flood of blessing (Psalm 85:1, Ezekiel 34:26, Malachi 3:10), a wave, or even a raging incoming tide (Isaiah 59:19, NLT). The outpouring of the Holy Spirit is one of the most dynamic pictures of God's sovereign descent on people in New Testament times (Acts 2:17,18,33; 10:45). Caught up in the picture of water is also its cleansing power, from sin and its dirtying effects, as signified in the waters of baptism.

Michael Green used this metaphor in his book about revivals in the UK, which he wrote in 2015, 'Not to put too fine a point on it, Christianity is in low water'.[6]

A movement in the Earth has been known to occur as part of God's working. In the days of the New Testament church, a vital prayer meeting in Jerusalem ended with an earth tremor that shook the exact place where the believers had gathered (Acts 4:31). The event was not regarded as any coincidence. A UK revival was once described as an earthquake by a Prime Minister who had lived through it (see chapter 7).

Something infectious is a metaphor that has led to the use of related words like 'caught' and 'outbreak'. Although not expressly a Bible metaphor, the way that revival has so often been caught from others makes this a metaphor that fits especially well in these recent times of pandemic. Revival can be spiritually infectious.

Link to the coronavirus (Covid-19) outbreak

From this point onwards, we will refer to this highly infectious virus simply as coronavirus, a less technical name for the disease causing the pandemic of 2020. It will be seen from several historical situations mentioned in this book that community trauma, as for instance caused by a health epidemic, have at times resulted in some level of revival. It is not surprising that shared trauma, where people's lives are threatened and some are lost, causes more individuals to start asking the important big questions of life like: Who am I? Where am I going? What am I here for? What is the point of life? Can all of life be described just in material terms? What is most important in my life? It was a personal trauma, the death of a dear friend, that got me asking those questions as a student.

Going more or less everywhere

God's footsteps can be traced just about everywhere from past revivals in the UK. If you wonder why so many different places are mentioned in this book, it is to help affirm that nowhere in the country has been too hard for God or beyond His notice. Some of the places mentioned should be already recognisable. Equally, some of the names of the people of God in past revivals should be recognisable too, and many others deserve to be known about as well.

Stylistic and content choices

Attention has been given wherever possible to explain how a particular move of God began, and who was involved humanly speaking. It can be seen that God has often been pleased to use young, or spiritually young, people for this.

There is a risk when presenting brief historical accounts, as in this book, of making past real-life events, people and situations seem simpler than they actually were. Therefore, some stories and events have been described here without a great deal of commentary. This will hopefully encourage readers to think, talk and seek out more about these accounts (e.g. What did motivate the minister Peter Price to criticise Evan Roberts so fiercely in the Welsh Revival in January 1905?).

Revival is only capitalised when part of a title or at the start of a sentence. Given the challenges of the great diversity of Christian leaders in this inter-denominational book, clerical titles (like 'the Rev.' meaning something different from 'the Revd.') have been left out when possible. No disrespect is intended by this. Bible quotations are from the New Living Translation (NLT) unless it is otherwise stated.

Revival in figures

There are different ways in which revival evidence can be measured. An immediately available figure has often been the number of conversions recorded at the time. This refers to the number of people who have publicly put their faith in Christ. These numbers seem fairly reliable in themselves, counted from people who identified themselves at the time. However, it is difficult to be sure what happened afterwards to all those 'converts', because they might have joined another church, or none, or left the region altogether.

A more reliable measure, when available, is given by the figures of church membership from one year to the next. The sources of these figures are typically in church or denominational records. At one end of the scale, the early Methodists kept very detailed records. At the other end, the Anglican church's numbers are much harder to make use of, because a person named on an Anglican church list can undergo profound changes of commitment without showing up any differently in the church's statistics. In some cases, the press reported on numbers of people, especially when the journalists were filing a positive report about what they had witnessed.

Thought for reflection

The people of God need to pray for revival – first and foremost in themselves.

Prayer

Lord, before I start longing for any more revival out there, please begin to revive me!

1

The Reformation as a revival and its Puritan legacy

Christ Jesus came into the world to save sinners.

(1 Timothy 1:15)

The Reformation in the British Isles was, of course, a political event as well as a religious one. Many books about it understandably focus on the political and personal power play involved rather than on what God was doing under the surface. While reforms of the church were needed, that is not the same as a revival of the church.

This chapter traces what led up to, and the legacy from, the revival that took place as a result of the Reformation. It essentially involved the common people reading the Bible and then responding to its life-imparting content. Perhaps most of all because of the major political dimension to the Reformation, this revival was attended by an immersion of suffering for many who either strongly supported or opposed it.

Forerunners of the Reformation

Some factors leading to the Reformation were the rise of literacy and also the recognition by the common people that they had some rights as well as obligations and, with it, the ability to think for themselves. Public attempts by the people to assert themselves were at first brutally put down, as in the rebellion under Simon de Montfort which ended in 1265 and the Peasants Revolt of 1381. The construction of the first printing presses in Europe, from 1450, was another vital prelude to the Reformation.

The greatest forerunner of the Reformation in England was John Wycliffe, born in the 1320s, who has been called 'the Morning Star of the Reformation'. His followers the Lollards later spread his thinking far and wide. A critical moment in his life was caused by a pandemic much worse than the Coronavirus one. Successive waves of the Black Death killed as many as 1 in 4 of the country's population in the fourteenth century. He saw the outbreak of the pandemic in 1348-1349 as a judgement of God. While he found peace and direction through reading *the Vulgate*, a fourth century Latin translation of the Bible, it made him realise how completely his countrymen were cut off from the Bible's teaching about God.

He rose to being the leading theologian at the University of Oxford, which must have helped protect him in the earlier stages as he spoke out about the need for church reforms. He saw the Bible as a necessary balance to the discredited authority of the church. He was the first person to organise and complete a translation of the Bible into English, from the Vulgate. He had strong affection for the poor, and he wanted the 'law of God' to be available to anyone who could read.

He was prominent enough that he appeared before Parliament in 1377 and gave them a defence of his alleged heresies ('wrong' beliefs). They went on to ask him his opinion on the question of withholding taxes to the Pope at that time. He declared it would be rank stupidity to send money to Rome when the country needed charity so urgently. It is clear that members of the Parliament were firmly on his side and against Rome.

It appears to have been the moment in 1378 when the Church of Rome inaugurated two Popes, one in Rome and one in Avignon, that prompted Wycliffe to publicly identify the Bible as the supreme source of spiritual authority. In 1382, any remaining tolerance towards him was lost after his attack on *transubstantiation* (the Roman Catholic teaching that the elements of bread and wine in communion become the real body and blood of Jesus). This practice was the very centre of the Roman church's priestly powers, so it was very important to them. He died in 1384, before he was officially denounced as a *heretic* (holding opinions opposed to traditional beliefs).

The Lollards responded to Wycliffe's teaching and example by dedicating themselves to secret group Bible reading. They went out and preached Wycliffe's ideas about being ruled by the Bible rather than by inherited tradition. In so doing, they helped to establish the idea that the common people could learn from the Bible in English without necessarily having priests involved.

A few of the Lollards were executed as heretics and many more gave way to pressure to recant (unsay) their Bible-based beliefs. Nonetheless, Lollard congregations continued to exist in various places until the time of the English Reformation.[1]

The Reformation in Europe

The flashpoint that started the Reformation occurred in 1517 when the monk Martin Luther nailed his 95 theses to the door of the castle church in Wittenberg. Luther was not actually pleading for an overall reformation of the church. He was pointing out the need for some detailed reforms, especially regarding the sale of so-called *indulgences* (claimed to reduce the length and severity of the punishment a person would pay for their sins) by the Church of Rome.

The furore that this rather academic dispute produced, rather than any penitence or details of possible reforms, caused Luther to realise in the following few years that a person is saved by faith and without works of the law (as in Romans 1:17). He concluded also that a complete reform of the Church was needed.

In general, the original German version of the Reformation (Lutheranism under Martin Luther) had less lasting effect in the British Isles than the Genevan version (Calvinism, or Reformed teaching, arising chiefly from the teaching of John Calvin).

France might have had its own full Reformation under Francois I, as he and Henry VIII were rather comparable characters. However, any prospect of agreement with Protestants in France turned later into fierce persecution of believers. As a direct result, in time Protestant England and Scotland were enriched by the presence and influence of many *Huguenot* exiles (French believers, also primed by Calvinism) who were fleeing the persecution unleashed against them in France.[2, 3]

The Reformation in England and Scotland

The first English translation from the Greek New Testament to reach England was written by Erasmus, a Dutch scholar. A Cambridge Fellow called Thomas Bilney read it. The words 'Christ Jesus came into the world to save sinners' (1 Timothy 1:15) caused Bilney to feel an immediate comfort and quietness. He found that reading the New Testament was even more pleasant than eating honey. He was no Lutheran because he was not in touch with them, and he helped to draw a number of others to the Reformation before being executed for his beliefs in 1531.

Printed writings by Luther began arriving in England (notably through Ipswich), a matter of delight for the descendants of the Lollards. After the Pope had condemned Luther, his writings were burned in Oxford, Cambridge and London. However, telling English people not to do something has long been a strong motivation for them to become interested in what has been forbidden, and the burning and banning of Luther's works just made his writings all the more popular.

The need for some secrecy also helped to foster the need for an underground network of Lutheran groups across the country. In Cambridge, the amount of pro-Luther talk over beer in the White Horse Tavern led to the nickname there of 'Little Germany'[4].

From 1526, copies of a New Testament translation by an Englishman called William Tyndale started flooding into the country from the Low Countries, hidden in merchandise. Some years previously, an exasperated Tyndale had said to a spiritually ignorant priest in England, "Ere [before] many years I will cause a boy that driveth the plough shall know more of the scriptures than thou dost."[5] He had set about being true to his word.

The translation quality of Tyndale's version of the Bible, though not fully completed by him, was very good. It was superseded in terms of fame by the King James Version (KJV), but the latter makes much use of his translation. He made his mark on English spelling, giving the language many spellings that are still in use today such as burden, most, mouth, prophets, sinners, theirs and when. His spelling of many Bible words became the accepted norm for later translators.

Tyndale wrote various other texts which were circulated too. Meanwhile, severe penalties were introduced in England against possession of scriptures and unauthorised preaching. That did not stop Anne Boleyn acquiring a copy of Tyndale's *The obedience of the Christian man*. She subsequently gave her copy to Henry, who read it with some appreciation.

Despite all the dangers that he and others faced, Tyndale managed to get 116,000 copies of the Bible into England before an English agent finally caught up with him, leading to his execution for heresy in 1536. The outward Reformation that Henry achieved was significantly made possible by the widespread support for the evangelical faith that had developed in response to the extensive circulation and reading of Tyndale's Bible. Tyndale's dying prayer was "Lord, open the King of England's eyes." It was only two years later that, in 1538, Henry VIII commanded – with Archbishop Cranmer's encouragement – that an English Bible should be made available in every parish church.[5]

Henry VIII's title Defender of the Faith (abbreviated to Fid. Def.), given to him by Pope Leo, is still used by British monarchs and on English coins. The other main European leaders of the day also had some title indicating their devotion to Jesus Christ, so such a grandiose title was far from unique. It was Bishop Gardiner who gave Henry the idea of retaining an independent Catholic church controlled by the Crown.

Henry VIII's only son, born to Anne Boleyn and later crowned Edward VI, was a true believer. In his short reign, Bible-based (that is, evangelical) beliefs flourished. He had clear views on the future of the English church. He helped to establish the church so far in a Protestant direction that his half-sister Mary was unable to reverse it more than temporarily after his early death in 1553. He also had a strong interest in education. Several grammar schools were founded in his name, some of which continue until now as King Edward VI schools.

Following the death of Henry VIII, Thomas Cranmer remained as Archbishop of Canterbury. He rewrote the Book of Common Prayer, published in 1552, which remains the foundation of Anglican church services of today.

Public preaching was done by men such as Hugh Latimer (who had been won over to the evangelical faith by Thomas Bilney), John Hooper (Bishop of Gloucester) and John Bradford (Prebendary of St. Paul's). This resulted in great interest and success. Open air gatherings at St. Paul's Cross in London brought together as many as 6,000 people at one time.[6]

When Queen Mary succeeded Edward VI, she immediately set about trying to return England to being a Roman Catholic country. She married Philip of Spain in 1554. Although welcomed by loyal Catholics in the land, Mary and Philip were never popular, and he did not stay long in England. In her reign, about 300 Christian leaders and others were burned at the stake because they would not renounce their Protestant faith. Consumed in the flames were men such as Cranmer, Latimer, Nicholas Ridley (Master of Pembroke Hall, Cambridge), Hooper and Bradford.

The death of each of these men was poignant. Latimer and Ridley were burned together at Oxford. A bag of gunpowder had been hung around their necks, and Latimer spoke words to Ridley that have been called his greatest ever sermon: "Be of good comfort, Master Ridley, and play the man. We shall this day light such a candle by God's grace in England as I trust shall never be put out!"[5,7]

Whatever remaining public goodwill and sympathy that was still left in England towards the old faith of Rome was finally extinguished at Mary's death in 1558 because of her unmerciful policies. She died childless. There remained, of course, individuals and households who were still firmly loyal to the Church of Rome. Mary's half-sister Elizabeth, the daughter of Anne Boleyn, is said to have responded when told she was now Queen, 'This is the Lord's doing and it is marvellous in our eyes.'"[5, 8]

Some 200 Christians had fled from Great Britain to Geneva, where they benefited greatly from the teaching of John Calvin, who was the greatest theologian of the Reformation. They also came under the renewed influence of the continental theologians Martin Bucer and Peter Martyr.

Among the Scottish exiles was John Knox. He had grown up in Haddington in East Lothian, which was one of the few towns where a broad education was possible in those days. He was a student in Glasgow and was ordained as a minister in about 1530. He embraced Protestant beliefs in middle age, partly through reading the works of Augustine, the early Church Father.

Knox was also deeply influenced by George Wishart, who had been banished from Scotland and was now back there instructing whoever would listen to him about Reformation teaching. Wishart did not live long doing that, as Cardinal Beaton had him tried, condemned and burned at the stake. Wishart preached his last sermon at Haddington. Knox might have gone on with him and been arrested soon afterwards, but Wishart persuaded him not to join him.

Shortly afterwards, some young men took over St. Andrew's Castle where Cardinal Beaton was, and Beaton was murdered. The castle then became a Protestant refuge for about a year, until it was taken back by a French force. In that time, Knox and some others from Haddington joined them.

Knox's speaking ability and his bold readiness to denounce the papacy were soon evident. Those present in the castle made him their minister, despite his reluctance to accept the position. The first ever communion held in the reformed manner in Scotland took place there. His prophetic ability was coldly reliable. When the French came and attacked the castle, he correctly foretold to the over-zealous reformers that it would be taken, saying that they could not escape the judgement of God.

Knox was then among those who were sent off to the French galleys, where he spent the next nineteen months 'chained to the oar'. That miserable experience permanently damaged his health but not his faith.

His uncompromising spirit was evident more than once. At one point, his companion James Balfour was so concerned about his health that he asked him if he knew where they were. Looking towards the shore and the towers of St. Andrew's, Knox identified it. He added that however weak he might now look, he would live to glorify God's name in that place. On another occasion, when he was ordered by the galley's officers to kiss an image of the Virgin Mary he just threw it overboard. He somehow survived doing that and was not challenged in a similar way again.

After his release from the galleys, Knox spent some time in England. He was a King's Chaplain, working under Cranmer on the wording of the church's 39 Articles that were composed in the reign of Edward VI. He was offered the opportunity to be made a bishop, but he refused it because he correctly foresaw that England would not favour him for long. Edward's untimely death in July 1553, followed by Mary's ascent to the throne, left Knox starving. He left England for the continent and reached Geneva. Including some time spent as a minister in Frankfurt, he was in Geneva until 1559. He was made the minister of an English-speaking church there too.[6, 9]

Return of the exiles from Geneva

The large majority of the 200 English-speaking exiles were able to return home after Elizabeth became Queen in November 1558. Knox was invited back to Scotland in 1559, which he reached in early May. Those who returned to England were called Puritans in the years that followed. The era of the English Puritans would last about a hundred years in all. Those who went to Scotland would be called *Covenanters*, because of the Covenant they made with each other affirming their common allegiance to God.

The causes of the Covenanters and the Puritans both prospered because of the same rising tide of revival in both realms. A school of preachers was formed in each. The Geneva Bible (1560) translation was so widely used that it had gone into 140 editions by 1644.

Elizabeth was well schooled in Protestant thinking because of the teaching she had received from Cranmer when she was a girl. However, now that England was again a Protestant nation, she generally regarded the Reformation as completed. The Christians who had returned to England were safe, but they found little sympathy from her towards their ideas of further reforms. Her peacemaking solution to all the past bloodshed, and the wide differences of views that had inspired it, was to have a tolerant church and people. Her policy goes far to explain both the traditionally tolerant style of the British people and the broad nature of the Anglican Church to this day.

Despite the peaceful resolutions of Elizabeth, the Pope excommunicated her. Political plots continued to surface that were intended to remove her from being Queen. What had begun as toleration towards the Catholic faith changed to it being a treasonable offence to remain loyal to the Church of Rome. There were many Catholic plots to depose or kill her. In addition, the violent intentions of Philip II in sending the Spanish Armada of 130 ships against Elizabeth and Protestant England are unmistakable. The Armada was prevented from landing and was then dispersed by atrocious weather conditions. It ended at the cost of many lives.

John Knox and his friend Christopher Goodman went back Scotland in 1559 because of an appeal for help from the Reformers there. It seemed that only Knox could bring the help that was needed. He preached first in Perth and then in St. Andrew's, true to his words that he had spoken while he was a galley slave. The Reformers in each place were transformed with new confidence.

Knox and those with him survived their initial success in Perth, despite the Queen Regent Mary of Guise heading for them with French troops. Mary was the widow of James V and the mother of the eight-year-old Mary Stuart who would later be known as Mary Queen of Scots. Know gained a strong enough bargaining position by boldly appealing to the nobles of Scotland to come and help him. After comparable success in St. Andrew's as he had seen in Perth, Knox and those with him set out for Edinburgh. Following the death of Mary of Guise in 1560, the French agreed that the Scottish Parliament could settle its own affairs on church matters, and they left with all their troops.

The Scottish Parliament met in August 1560. It declared with a large majority that Scotland was a Protestant nation and that the Pope no longer had any authority there. Scottish patriotism against the French, who had seemed to be taking the country over, merged with Scottish Protestantism. The first Assembly of the Church of Scotland met on 20th December. All matters of Christian teaching and practice had to conform to a new confession of faith drawn up by John Knox. Scotland became a Calvinist country because the people rather than the monarch wanted it.

Knox and others saw remarkable levels of response to their preaching. John Knox House in the Royal Mile in Edinburgh is well worth a visit, showing where Knox lived until his death in 1572.

Revival in Scotland became general in those intervening years. Except for the Highlands, which remained largely Catholic, the people of Scotland embraced the Protestant faith at every level of society, to an extent that almost no other nation has seen. The Scottish church was relatively independent already and was not held back from reforms needed to help change it from its pre-Reformation condition.[6, 9]

The Reformation in Ireland

The Reformation largely failed to take root in Ireland, except in Ulster and in some cities like Dublin where English rule was strongest. Ireland was the only country in Europe not to adopt the Reformation when its ruler did so. Perhaps the reason for this was that the English attempted to impose the Reformation there too much like a top-down political change. The large majority in Ireland remained loyal to Roman Catholicism, and this had consequences regarding how receptive the people and the clergy of the southern provinces were to revival in the following centuries.

The Reformation in Wales

The Reformation in England resulted in some English preachers appearing in the border areas. The Bible was later translated into Welsh by William Morgan, and was published in 1588. That made it all the easier for the gospel to be explained in Welsh also. There were strong differences of loyalty, leading some people to remain with the Church of Rome. The welcome given to the gospel by some Welsh (Celtic) people, though, indicates that it was not that the Reformation was unattractive to Celts, as might be interpreted from its relative rejection in Ireland.

James I

James VI of Scotland was invited at the time of Elizabeth's death to be King of England as well as Scotland, making him James I of England and Ireland. He had no sympathy with the experimental godliness that was typical of the

Covenanters, and he passed on to his children (including Charles, his successor) a sense of their god-like status. James found the hierarchical structure of the Church of England, led by bishops, considerably easier to control and govern than the Presbyterian Church of Scotland where churches were more independent and led jointly by elders.

James I's greatest spiritual contribution was the commissioning of a new translation of the Bible, now known as the King James Version (KJV) or Authorised Version (AV). It is the most famous ever English translation of the Bible. The six translation committees, drawn together to do the translation in different locations, made good use of Tyndale's translation which had been completed after his death by John Rogers and Miles Coverdale.

The KJV is regarded as being on a level with the works of Shakespeare for the scale of its influence on the development of the English language. Melvyn Bragg, the broadcaster and parliamentarian, made the case at the time of the 400th anniversary of the KJV in 2011 that the Bible is one of the fundamental makers of the modern world and that it inspired democracy, social reform and *emancipation* (setting people free).[10]

Although not immediately obvious to the casual reader, the beautiful language of the KJV reflects James' intent to help underpin the existing (Episcopal) form of church government in England. For example, it uses a word like 'bishop' rather than 'overseer' or 'elder' which would have been a more accurate translation of the respective Greek words *episkopos* and *presbuteros*. In Acts 12:4, what should have been worded as 'Passover' was translated as 'Easter'.

Some English Puritans, now called the Pilgrims, were all too aware of the limitations of religious freedom in England under James I. 102 passengers and a crew of 30 sailed the Atlantic on the Mayflower for the New World in 1620. The result was the birth of a new nation that would have an important part in future revivals.

The Universities

Cambridge (previously dubbed 'Little Germany') became the most formative place for the Reformation in England. The great preachers there included Thomas Cartwright, William Perkins, Laurence Chaderton and Richard Sibbes. Samuel Clarke said of Perkins, who regularly preached at St. Andrew's church (now known as St. Andrew the Great), that he 'held forth a burning and shining light, the sparks whereof did fly abroad into all the corners of the kingdom.'[6]

The work of God there was also furthered by the foundation of Emmanuel College in 1584 'to render as many as possible fit for the administration of the Divine Word and Sacraments'. Chaderton, its Master, was succeeded in 1622 by John Preston, another Puritan. Perkins was a fellow of Christ's College. Sibbes came back to Cambridge from London to be Master of St. Katherine's College in 1626. One of his fellows Thomas Goodwin described the high-tide nature of England at that time: 'if in any age or in any coast it is or hath been full tide, it is now in England.'

In Oxford, there was a high tide of spiritual life during the time of the Commonwealth. Oxford became comparable to what Cambridge had been like in earlier years, due mainly to the preaching of Thomas Goodwin and John Owen.[6]

The English Civil War and the Commonwealth

Charles I claimed divine kingship without subservience to anyone, which can be seen with hindsight to have set him on a collision course with the English Parliament. Their irreconcilable differences led to the Civil War between them. The Parliamentarian side, as the war progressed, came under Oliver Cromwell's highly effective military leadership. It could be said broadly that the Puritans helped to win the war and then, for various reasons, lost the peace that followed it during the Commonwealth.

The Restoration

The Commonwealth did not last more than two years after the death of Oliver Cromwell. Some Puritan preachers could be very direct in their criticisms of the King. Charles II would have needed little reminding anyway that it was under Puritan leadership that his father had been dethroned and later executed, and himself nearly captured. Successive Acts of Parliament in the early years of the Restoration were clearly designed to remove Puritans, wherever possible, from public and church life.[11]

Puritan preachers and writers

Besides founding a new nation across the Atlantic, the Puritans gave the world a number of outstanding preachers and writers. They helped to foster a developing robustness in the character of the English people, which caused them to make an enormous contribution to political freedom in the country. They were so firm in their beliefs that they were often lacking in agreement with each other.

John Rogers (*c.* 1570-1636) preached with such awakening power that it was still being spoken of a century later. His dramatised way of speaking captured the attention of his hearers. For example, he once pretended to be God speaking to the congregation and threatening to take away their Bible because they were neglecting it. Then he pretended to be the congregation giving their answer back to God. Decades later, when revival had taken hold in America, some English critics took offence at what they heard about public shows of grief and conviction among the hearers. An old man called Timothy Edwards reminded them how common that same response had been in the days of John Rogers.

Matthew Henry (1662-1714) spent much of his ministerial life in Chester, mainly as a Presbyterian. Despite recurring ill health, Henry set about writing a whole commentary of the Bible. The full work was not completed by the time of his death, and it was finished with the contributions of 13 other ministers. Published in 6 volumes, his is one of the greatest of commentaries of the whole Bible. One of his practices was to pray through a verse of Psalm 119 every day, giving him time to pray through the whole psalm twice in a year. He was the author and exemplar of the much-quoted words commenting on Zechariah 12:10, 'When God intends great mercy for his people, the first thing he does is to set them a praying.'[12, 13]

John Milton (1608-1674) was a poet and intellectual. He was employed as a civil servant during the Commonwealth. His epic poem *Paradise Lost* is considered to be one of the greatest works of all English literature.

Richard Baxter (1615-1691) was a highly impressive thinker, writer and Anglican minister. During his nearly two decades as Vicar at St. Mary and All Saints in Kidderminster, in Worcestershire, almost the entire community came to a personal faith in Christ. This happened partly through his systematic visiting and teaching of people in their own homes. He wrote one of the first ever *evangelistic* books (telling others about Jesus). 20,000 copies of *A Call to the Unconverted*, were sold in its first year, and it helped to lead a huge stream of readers to Christ. He wrote over 130 books in all.

John Bunyan (1628-1688) was a fiery Baptist preacher capable of attracting audiences of a thousand. He was imprisoned in Bedford jail for preaching without a (Anglican church) licence. His 'crime' was the result of one of the laws brought in against Puritans. He wrote the spiritual allegory *A Pilgrim's Progress* as a serialised story to read to his blind daughter when she visited him in prison. This book is considered to be one of the greatest works of Christian fiction, made possible because of what a popular preacher did in a long-extended lockdown. Only the Bible has sold more copies than this book.

The Westminster Assembly, which began in 1643, was intended to reform the English church. It brought together both English and Scottish ministers and theologians. They were united enough to produce *The Westminster Confession*, a statement of faith that is still used today.[6]

A local revival at the Kirk of Shotts

One of the most remarkable local revivals happened at the Kirk of Shotts, a town in North Lanarkshire, in 1630. John Livingston, a powerful young preacher of 27 was invited to address a large outdoor assembly on sloping ground west of the Kirk (church) on the Monday following the large gathering for a Communion Sunday.

Some people had spent the night beforehand praying and talking to each other. Livingston preached from Ezekiel 36:25-26, which includes such memorable words as 'a new heart I will give you'. He spoke very well throughout, as later testimony showed. However, the unplanned crisis of his long message came as a result of a shower of rain. As the congregation began to draw their cloaks more securely around them, Livingston commented what a mercy it was that God should shower rain upon them rather than the fire and brimstone that He had done upon Sodom and Gomorrah.

Livingston's very Scottish observation cut his listeners to the heart. A remarkable manifestation of feeling could be seen among the listeners, which his own conversion and experience of revival helped him to recognise. Some were struck down still upon the ground so long that friends and others began to wonder if they were still alive. About 500 people experienced a saving change in their lives that day, and the revival then spread over the whole surrounding area.[14]

Some consequences of the Reformation

The English-speaking people gained the Bible in their mother tongue. Early Modern English was formed with countless Christian characteristics embedded in it. This could give some explanation of why so many people have found faith through the versatile world language of English in the intervening centuries.

The nations of England and Scotland (except the Highlands) became clearly Protestant. Following so much bloodshed, an attitude of broad toleration and an ability to cope with many differences around them has pervaded their behaviour until at least the challenges of the recent past.

A new nation was founded in the New World, starting off with Jesus Christ at its centre.

Thought for Reflection

When God intends great mercy for his people, He first of all sets them a-praying. (Matthew Henry commenting on Zechariah 12:10)

Prayer

Lord, please help me to pray all the better for You to move in power in the United Kingdom.

2

The Evangelical Awakening

I tell you the truth, unless you are born again, you cannot see the Kingdom of God.

(John 3:3)

A low spiritual state

It is difficult to imagine what a low moral state the United Kingdom, and its colonies, had fallen into in the first quarter of the eighteenth century.

At the time, the Anglican church was led largely by ministers who had little spiritual life in them. The legal measures taken under Charles II in the previous century to exclude the Puritans from public and church life had had their intended effect, leaving the Anglican church largely in the hands of those who cared more about the forms of Christianity than its spirit. Many ministers were absent from their posts.

In terms of their social background, most clergy belonged broadly to the same 'gentry' class as the local landowners. Many clerical positions were appointed by local landowners, and bishops were appointed to their position by the Government. A bishop held a position that was little different from being part of the civic authorities.

One of the outstanding *dissenting* (non-Anglican) ministers of the day was Philip Doddridge. In April 1729, he organised a 'day of humiliation and prayer for religious revival' with his fellow Congregationalist ministers in Lutterworth.[1] God heard the words of their prayer meeting, but probably not in the way that those praying might have expected.

A weakened church left the country open to all kinds of behaviours and dangers. The Treaty of Utrecht (1713) gave Britain main control over the slave trade. The brutality of that way of making so much money, at the cost of Africans who were considered less than human, must have hardened consciences and reduced people's sensitivity in many ways. There were 160 crimes attracting the death penalty, with application to men, women and children.

Alcohol consumption had increased to dangerous levels. A law in 1689 had outlawed the importation of spirits, therefore stopping the import of brandy from France. That led to the opening of gin distilleries in people's homes. It reached a point where one city home in six might be a gin shop, and gin was very cheap. Over-drinking of alcohol not only led to greater criminality but it was killing off people so fast that the author Henry Fielding commented in 1751 that, within 20 years, there would be very few of the common people left to drink it.

This was when the famous satirical prints by William Hogarth were published, called 'Beer Street' and 'Gin Lane'. Hogarth drew the pictures in support of what would be called the Gin Act (1751). The new law finally banned all the small-scale distillation of spirits.

Dangers from thieves and highwaymen meant that many travellers were robbed. The politician Horace Walpole wrote in 1751 that you set out to travel, even at noon, as if armed for battle.

Besides heavy drinking, favourite pastimes of the day included gambling, cock fighting (a fight to the death), *prize fighting* (bare-knuckle boxing) and attendance at public executions. Team games were rare, and cruelty to animals was commonplace.

At that time there was also one of the worst financial scandals in the nation's history, called the South Sea Bubble. With the *connivance* (support in wrongdoing) of the Government and the use of payments to supporters, a company was created in 1711 that gave exclusive trading rights to the South Sea Company to trade with Spanish colonies and the West Indies. In fact, no agreement had been made with the Spanish to trade with them, and the trading company had no ships. The company's primary function was really about funding government debt.

An investment frenzy in 1720 pushed the company's share price up to an unsustainable level. Finally the bubble burst, causing the financial ruin of many and disgrace for several politicians. The scheme has been the byword ever since for many another 'bubble' since then. The South Sea Bubble episode remains as a national monument to human and financial folly.[2]

How revival happened

Revival came to Wales in the generation before it began in England. Wales had a much smaller population than England and was a relatively poor part of the country. Mining was one of few forms of employment available besides working on the land.

Griffith Jones was a minister who went around preaching, with great success, in and beyond his parish of Llanddowror in Carmarthenshire from 1716 onwards. He also established *circulating schools* that, within one generation, reached 158,237 children and adults throughout Wales.[2] These circulating, Welsh-speaking, schools were based in a given location for three months before moving on. The Bible was a textbook in these schools, so the Welsh population steadily came to understand the message of Christianity. As had happened in England in the Reformation, reading of the scriptures was a key preparation for the revival that followed. Jones has been called 'the Morning Star' of the Great Awakening.

One day in the early 1730s, Jones was preaching in a village where he was so struck by the scoffing attitude of a young Anglican minister, called Daniel Rowland, that he quietly prayed that the young man's heart might be changed. Rowland was indeed converted and was further transformed by repeated spiritual visitations of God to his congregation in Llangeitho, in what is now the county of Dyfed. He was an outstanding preacher, and he became a Methodist after his bishop deprived him of his curacy in the parish. His supporters built him a chapel in Llangeitho, and most of the congregation joined him there. On communion Sundays, he preached out of doors to thousands of people. An associate of Rowland was Hywel (Howell) Harris, who travelled around Wales spreading the gospel.[3]

The revival in England can be traced back primarily not so much to these events in Wales as to a revival overseas in a place called Herrnhut (meaning 'the Lord's watch') in Germany. The landowner, Count von Zinzendorf, was a Christian man whom God had been working in deeply from childhood. He allowed some of his land to be settled on by a small, persecuted group of Christians from Moravia, located in what is now part of the Czech Republic.

Under von Zinzendorf's dynamic leadership, a church developed in which the people, including the Count himself, were most thoroughly revived. They reached a moment in August 1727 when those present compared their experience to that of the Holy Spirit coming down at Pentecost. It was the beginnings of a new denomination, known as the Moravian Church.

The Moravians became greatly concerned for people of the world lost without God and they started to send out people in pairs to take them the gospel of Jesus Christ. They began a prayer meeting that continued 24/7 for 100 years. People in the prayer team took hourly times to pray within each 24 hours. The first mission in 1732 involved sending out two men to take the gospel to black slaves in the West Indies. Before long, others went out from Herrnhut to various destinations, including London.

In the next 30 years, that little Moravian community sent out 600 missionaries. Some of them sailed to America in

1737, in order to take the gospel to Native Americans. As it happened, there was also an English clergyman on board. Through the later work of these Moravians, revival took place in some of the American colonies. The most noteworthy minister from those early days of revival in America was Jonathan Edwards, who is nowadays regarded by many as the greatest of all revival theologians.[2]

John Wesley

The clergyman who the Moravians met was a former university tutor called John Wesley. His subsequent service as a chaplain to British colonists in the new colony of Georgia was fairly disastrous. The woman who he loved married another man. His congregation rebelled against the group disciplines that he had tried to impose upon them.

It had been evident at the University of Oxford, where he had been a Fellow of Lincoln College, that Wesley was a born leader. He formed there a little group of like-minded religious young men, who were so disciplined and full of good deeds that they attracted various nicknames. These included 'the Holy Club' and 'Bible-moths'. Somebody even thought of calling them 'Methodists', as there was so much tireless method in their behaviour. The group included Charles, John's younger brother and, later on, George Whitefield.

John Wesley had known from a very young age that God had some special role for him in life. His parents were both descended from Puritan ministers who had been made to leave the Anglican church. His father Samuel and his mother Susannah had both become Anglicans by choice.

Susannah was the mother of 19 children, though only about 6 of them reached adulthood. She must have been good at delegating tasks to the older ones: when she wanted to pray, she would just sit in her chair and pull her apron over her head. The ability to pray privately and regularly, even when surrounded by others, was learned from her example. She also taught her children how to rise above mockery, which must have done much to help John and Charles when at Oxford and in later life.

Their father Samuel's style of Bible-oriented ministry in the parish church in Epworth was forthright and clearly lacked some of the grace that his sons John and Charles would later discover. It was not well received by everyone in Epworth. It was probably no accident that the family home caught fire in February 1709.

That day in 1709 would be a critical one in Wesley's life. Everyone got out of the burning house safely, or so it seemed until they realised that young John was not among them. He was seen standing at an upper window, as the flames were taking hold everywhere. Some of the village bystanders climbed up and helped to pull the young boy from the open window shortly before the roof crashed down. For the rest of his life, Wesley thought of himself as a 'brand plucked out of the fire', as in Zechariah 3:2 (KJV).

We have already noted that in 1737, as Wesley was taking ship to America from England, he met a group of Moravians. His lifelong diaries or 'journals' had begun from the start of that voyage. The piety, simplicity and the group devotions of those 26 Moravians on board impressed him. He started learning German in order to talk to them, and they started to learn English.

A severe test came when the ship hit a bad storm in mid-Atlantic and was at risk of sinking. Wesley was deeply affected by the Moravians' profound faith and calm in the face of possible death. Wesley talked after that episode to the leader David Nitschmann, one of the first two Moravian missionaries, who asked him in reply if he had faith in Christ. Wesley noted in his diary that he replied that he did but that 'I fear these were vain words'.

When back in England in 1738, Wesley wrote in his diary 'But what have I learnt myself in the meantime? Why, – what I the least of all suspected, – that I, who went to America to convert others, was never myself converted to God.' When finally he went to London, he sought out the Moravians who were based there.

Less than four months after his return from Georgia, Wesley reluctantly attended a Moravian evening prayer meeting in Aldersgate Street. Someone read from Luther's Preface to the Apostle Paul's letter to the Romans, in which Luther described the change in the heart that happens to someone who has put their faith in Christ. As Wesley listened:

> *I felt my heart strangely warmed; I felt I did trust in Christ, Christ alone, for my salvation: and an assurance was given me that He had taken away my sins, even mine, and saved me from the law of sin and death. I began to pray with all my might ... I then testified openly to all there what I now first felt in my heart'.*[4]

Wesley's conversion was one of the most consequential in all of church history, commemorated today by a bronze memorial near the Museum of London. The manner of his conversion helped impress upon him the central importance of people being 'born again'.

Wesley's sharing of his new-found faith in his sermons was not well received. Churches that had been open to him while he was seeking clearer faith were no longer open to him now that he had found it. His friend George Whitefield helped him to get started doing open-air preaching.

Wesley preached later to any number who could be assembled to listen, whether in a small courtyard or in large open spaces where the acoustics were good enough. One of his favourite, and still visitable, preaching places was at Gwennap in Cornwall. Gwenapp Pit is an atmospheric amphitheatre at which he spoke to thousands.

He went to Scotland 22 times in all. At times his audiences were deeply moved, and methodist 'societies' were formed successfully in various places. However, the fruit from his work in Scotland was much less than in England and Wales.[4]

He taught a great deal and put a huge amount of his teaching in print. He encouraged his itinerant preachers to read for no less than 5 hours a day. He wrote 233 books and pamphlets, and helped with the writing of more than a hundred others. He preached about 45,000 sermons and travelled around the country a distance equivalent to going 9 times around the world.[5]

As well as reaching many through his publications, Wesley made a lasting impact by establishing small societies where he had been. These societies were the forerunners of 'class meetings' of local believers that he later set up. Members were made accountable for their walk with God in the previous week. It cost very little to join the class meeting, a charge to be covered by the group leader if the person concerned had no money. The required terms of belief were very simple, but the challenges to the will would be demanding.

One of Wesley's great topics was personal holiness. Another was education, and wherever Methodism was established a love of education and schooling followed. His saying on money is particularly famous. It was that Christians should 'Earn all you can, give all you can, save all you can.' He advised his followers not to spend undue amounts on themselves, such as on clothing, when money was so greatly needed to help the poor. He never did get on well with the very rich.

Like the others, Wesley reported on remarkable manifestations among some people in his audiences. Some people fell to the ground as if struck by lightning, some shook, while others roared, screamed, or fell down with involuntary laughter.

He lived a fruitful ministry up to the end of his life in 1791. A visit to Wesley's Chapel in City Road, London, where he is buried, can show his surroundings in the last, more settled years of his ministry. By then, the spiritual tide in the country that had been so against him had already turned. Many ministers and congregations were eager to come out and hear him if he came to speak nearby.[5, 6]

If John Wesley was the greatest congregation builder in the group and George Whitefield was its greatest speaker, Charles was its greatest hymn writer. Charles wrote about 6,500 of them. Some are still sung with enthusiasm today, including 'And can it be'. Invariably in the singing of it, this verse stands out strongly:

Long my imprisoned spirit lay
Fast bound in sin and nature's night;
Thine eye diffused a quickening ray
I woke, the dungeon flamed with light;
My chains fell off, my heart was free;
I rose, went forth, and followed Thee.

Charles and John were both hymn writers because they realised how singing could revitalise what people believed. It is perhaps due more to them than anyone else that revival first came to be associated with singing. Charles did open air preaching, and it was his chief activity for 16 years.[7] Like George Whitefield and his brother John, Charles and his preaching companions occasionally had some very difficult moments because of bitter opposition from mobs, perhaps worst of all in Devizes and Dublin. In Dublin, he and others were stoned and he was hit by a blow. On some occasions, he managed to calm down the leading opponents so well that they then became some of his chief defenders.

The mobs that the methodists encountered were not simply sudden expressions of community resistance. It was more the case that some people with wealth or influence were resistant enough to arouse a mob. A violent group could be put down by the local authorities, but that might not happen if those in authority objected to the methodists.

Charles faced stone throwing many times over, learning to trust in God's providence to bring him and his companions through alive. When he stood on the steps of the Market House in Walsall in 1743, stones were thrown at him repeatedly. Many of the stones struck him, but without unduly hurting him. He bade those responsible to be reconciled to God in Christ. It seemed as if a band of ruffians wanted to drag him away, but he resolutely stayed to finish his message. When he did so, he bade his audience to depart in peace and he walked away through the thickest groups of the rioters.

In 1744, hundreds of Methodist homes were damaged and looted by a rampaging mob in Wednesbury, near Walsall. In 1765, in North Taunton, a pack of hounds were set on the methodists, but the hounds became entirely quiet.

Neither Charles nor John paid for their courageous preaching with their lives. Charles Wesley died three years before his brother, in 1788, and was buried in the graveyard of Marylebone parish church in London.

A very small number of methodists died directly as a result of mob violence, such as a Mrs Baker and a financier called William Seward. Some itinerant preachers went to an early grave because of the injuries they had previously received. In contrast, the national government never resisted the revival.[6, 7]

George Whitefield

George Whitefield grew up in Gloucester. He was not especially interested in spiritual matters as a boy, but he loved the theatre. He became so good at theatrical practices that he even missed school to do more of them.

He found faith in Christ through seeking God with the help of the Holy Group in Oxford. He was socially and financially below the level of the others in the group, as the only way he could work his way through his studies at Oxford was to earn money as a servant to richer students.

Once he had put his faith in Christ, Whitefield found that audiences were drawn to listen to him as to a magnet. Like Wesley he too went off to America, though only for three months. On his return, he found pulpits closed against him, so that led him to start doing open air preaching. Though not particularly tall he was, like John Wesley, a giant of a preacher. He was an emotional and theatrical speaker, and a warm-hearted man. The famous actor David Garrick (1717-1779) is later said to have joked "I would give a hundred guineas [that was £105, worth vastly more today] to be able to say "Oh!" like Mr. Whitefield."

Whitefield's first main success was in open air preaching to miners at Kingswood, near Bristol. He went there after being told about it in Bristol. Why go to the Indians in America, he was asked, when there are colliers enough in Kingswood? The miners there were some of the most lawless and hardened labouring men anywhere, who might now be seen as some of the worst-treated victims of the Industrial Revolution. There was no local Anglican minister to annoy there, because the area of Kingswood did not have a church.

George, John and other preachers would later address many other types of poor working people, but this was one of the toughest audiences imaginable to start with. As he preached to the assembled audience of miners, on several occasions and to growing numbers, Whitefield knew he was getting through because of the lines of tears he could see washing down their blackened faces.

He was also very warmly received in Scotland, and it was there that the greatest of all his preaching events happened, in Cambuslang, on the south-eastern side of Glasgow. He had preached in Glasgow before, but he went to Cambuslang for the first time in July 1742. He recorded what happened after he preached three times in one day in a place that came to be called the Preaching Braes, a natural amphitheatre.

> *Such a commotion surely was never heard of, especially at eleven at night. It far outdid all that I ever saw in America. For about an hour and a half there was such weeping, so many falling into deep distress, and expressing it various ways... Their cries and agonies were exceedingly affecting. Mr. McCulloch preached after I had ended, till past one in the morning, and then could scarce persuade them to depart.*[7]

It was estimated on the following Sunday that 20,000 people took communion together outside. Whitefield was persuaded to return a month later and then, it was estimated, 30,000 people were in attendance.

He was also well received in Wales, where he and John Wesley were impressed by Griffith Jones and Daniel Rowland. Hywel Harris and William Williams, the hymn writer, also became part of Whitefield's connections there. From this group came the denomination known as Calvinistic Methodists.

Whitefield was not afraid to face controversy if it helped to draw a crowd, unlike the more measured but still passionate and direct style of John Wesley. Whitefield was willing to take the opportunities available to preach the gospel in the drawing rooms of the rich and powerful. When hearing the gospel explained in such a peaceable environment, many people of high social rank became lifelong followers of Christ. It is part of the wonder of the Evangelical Awakening that every class of British society was reached successfully.

An important and far-reaching difference between himself and John Wesley was that Wesley was much more of an organiser. Wesley was more conscious of his legacy, as evidenced by his 50 years of diary writing, and he proved rather capable of organising Whitefield's followers to become his own instead. Whitefield was more of a man for his own generation, ever keen to go and preach the gospel to yet more audiences rather than stay home and give pastoral care to those assembling under his influence.

He preached in nearly every main town in England, Scotland and Wales. He also found very willing audiences in America. He went to America a total of 7 times, beginning in 1739, and he met Jonathan Edwards there as a result of writing to him from New York on one such visit. While he was in America, his alienation from Anglican clergy who opposed him drew him into close fellowship with ministers of Presbyterian, Dutch Reformed and Baptist churches. After that, his work became more non-denominational in character.

A yet more important difference with John Wesley was a theological issue, about important aspects of grace. Wesley became a champion of *free grace*, which emphasises the free choice of the individual to respond fully to the grace of God being offered. He also maintained that a believer could attain full sanctification (full separation from evil things and ways) in this life. Whitefield took a more 'Calvinist' or 'Reformed' view, which emphasised the overarching part that God plays in a person's faith and life. The so-called 'Arminian' thinking of John Wesley set him at odds with the beliefs of people like Whitefield.

In the briefest terms, *Arminianism* emphasises the ability of people to respond to God's grace as they choose: they can accept it or reject it. This is at odds with *Reformed/ Calvinistic* teaching, which emphasises divine election (His choice) and the incapacity of the natural man or woman for true faith and repentance.

A new believer might hardly notice or understand the differences at first between these matters. However, cutting as it did to the heart of their preaching, these differences caused the two men to stop working in co-operation with each other.

At the level where individuals make an effort to achieve reconciliation with another person, never mind who is in the right, the available evidence indicates that Whitefield was the more conciliating person and John was the more uncompromising one.

Whitefield preached an estimated 18,000 times in his relatively short lifetime of 56 years. He died while on a preaching tour in America in September 1770. While his body had become weaker over the months before that, he had kept going. He was buried where he died, in Newburyport, Massachusetts.[8]

Selina Countess of Huntingdon

Selina, the Countess of Huntingdon, was a remarkable woman who acted on her own initiative in the work of revivals. Her husband, the 9th Earl of Huntingdon, was not closely identified with her religious activities, though he did not obstruct them.

An apparent hindrance to the spread of the revival was the parish system of the Anglican church, because any parish priest could, and with some legal force, object strongly to having uninvited Anglican preachers in his parish. John Wesley famously said "The world is my parish", but that did not silence unwelcoming parish priests.

The Countess realised that she could build a chapel wherever she owned or bought a property, and she could then have the final say about all the services and staff in those chapels. She established 64 chapels across England and Ireland, some of them large. These chapels formed a group, called 'The Countess of Huntingdon's Connexion'. Her influence on the revival was great. The Connexion is a denomination that exists to this day, both in the UK and in Sierra Leone.

One of the chapels was built, in part of the former village, in what are now called the Lanes in Brighton. The only surviving chapel of her own designs is in Bath. Built in 1765, it is open to the public as The Museum of Bath Architecture, at the Countess of Huntingdon's Chapel. It is easy to imagine there the Countess welcoming John Wesley and George Whitefield through the doors in the heyday of their partnership in the gospel.

In the parting of the ways between John Wesley and Whitefield, the Countess took the Calvinist (or 'Reformed') position favoured by Whitefield, so he remained a welcome preacher in her chapels and the many drawing room meetings that she helped to organise.[6, 9]

Co-workers in the Awakening

A revival that was so far-reaching geographically across the country required the raising up of many travelling preachers. One of the most famous to be associated with the methodists was Rowland Hill, who went on to found and pastor the free church Surrey Chapel in London.

One of the few Anglican clergy favourable to the revival was Thomas Grimshaw, who was a 'permanent curate' at Haworth in North Yorkshire. Hardly anyone attended church when he arrived in the village, but the numbers soon grew to hundreds. He got on so well with John Wesley that he was appointed his successor if he should die young. In fact, Grimshaw died many years before Wesley. Unfortunately, the international fame of the Brontë family who lived there in the next century has left William Grimshaw rather forgotten in comparison.[10]

Some consequences of the Evangelical Awakening

At the time of the death of John Wesley, the methodist movement had 71,668 followers, 294 preachers, 19 missionaries and 8,000 leaders in the British Isles.[6] They were well spread out across the country. In order to support the work better in America, he was obliged to appoint a superintendent who could ordain new leaders there. He appointed Thomas Coke, which in Anglican terms was almost like appointing a bishop. The use of that authority is seen as one key factor in why the methodist movement eventually broke away from the Anglican church, though in Wesley's lifetime he always protested their loyalty to it.

A far greater number of people attended one or more methodist meetings than those who became methodists. When the tide comes in, all the boats will rise, as the saying goes. Church attendance went up markedly in the denominations where members were encouraged to go and listen to the visiting methodist speakers. Wesley's enormous output of writing meant that his teaching, thinking and version of events lived on strongly long after his death.

In the mid-eighteenth century, most people in the Highlands and Islands of Scotland only spoke Gaelic. Therefore, the Society in Scotland for the Propagation of Christian Knowledge (SSPCK) started a translation project in 1755, to produce a version of the Bible in Scottish Gaelic. This resulted in the publication of the New Testament in 1767 and the whole Bible in 1801.

It is widely believed that the Evangelical Awakening helped to stave off the country from going down the path of revolution, rather than following the example of the French Revolution that began in 1789. It has already been described what a low and depressed state the country had been in during the previous decades. King George IV, who was the king in the final part of the eighteenth century, was far from being an ideal or popular monarch.

The self-serving attitudes of many landowners towards their people, as that of many of the new masters of emerging industries, help us understand the social conditions (including slavery) of the day, which the methodists addressed both powerfully and creatively. Wrong attitudes among the wealthy towards those their employees did not suddenly go away as a result of the revival. Important social improvements followed the Evangelical Awakening, and it was a theme that absorbed some great Christian efforts in the next two generations after the death of John Wesley.

Despite his radical bravery in opposing sinful practices and arguing for real holiness, John Wesley was a loyal subject of the Crown and a firm supporter of the government of the day. Any talk of *sedition* (insurrection and disorder against the state), of which there was plenty at that time, would be firmly squashed wherever the methodists went.

Wider impacts of the revival

The effect of methodism on the country was great. In 1922, the Prime Minister David Lloyd George spoke very appreciatively of the social transformation it achieved:

> *The movement which improved the conditions of the working classes, in wages, in hours of labour, and otherwise, found most of its best officers and non-commissioned officers, in men trained in institutions that were the result of Methodism… John Wesley inaugurated a movement that gripped the soul of England, that deepened its spiritual instincts, trained them and uplifted them.*[11]

The need for personal conversion was emphasised very clearly in the Evangelical Awakening. Even to this day, it is a foible of British citizens that many wrongly believe that any entrance to heaven must be earned to some extent by their own good deeds, despite the New Testament clearly teaching the opposite (Ephesians 2:8-9).

The impact of early methodist teaching and influence went out worldwide. Methodists in the American colonies at the time of the death of John Wesley numbered over 40,000. Many lively Christian denominations and groups functioning today still lay great importance on this.

The Evangelical Awakening retained much of what the Reformation had achieved. Wesley's campaigns, such as being against slavery and excessive drinking and for the education of unschooled children set new precedents for Christians seeking to change society that have carried on until now.

There was a memorable 'handing on of the relay baton' in the final weeks of John Wesley's life. He had himself campaigned strongly against slavery and written a paper against it in 1773, entitled *Thoughts upon Slavery*. His last letter was to the Christian politician William Wilberforce, who he had previously met. In it, he encouraged him to persevere in the fight against slavery. The scene was set for the well-known battle for social reform in the generation that followed his long and fruitful life.[2]

Thought for Reflection

A small group of Christians set in motion a movement that changed the nation and influenced many other parts of the world.

Prayer

Please help me/us to face even strong opposition when bringing the gospel to the nation.

3

Aftermath of the Evangelical Awakening

Am I not a man and a brother?
(inscription on Wedgewood cameo)

It would be easy to imagine that the incoming tide of revival in the eighteenth century continued steadily at least until the death of John Wesley in 1791. In fact, the pace of the revival slowed before then. Ongoing wars with the French set the politics of the UK into a fragile state, where anyone championing the poor and the underprivileged (including slaves) might be accused of siding with the French.

The country already had revived church ministers in every part of it, as a result of the Great Awakening, and fresh floods of revival appeared in separate places.

Revival in England

Despite the many spiritual and social changes that the Evangelical Awakening had set in motion, it was still running against the main philosophy of that time, which was Deism. *Deism* is a very undemanding form of religion, still with its descendants today. Reason and the observation of material things are seen as sufficient evidence to establish the existence of God.

Deism, while serious about the performance of ceremonies and church structures to honour God, can produce a rather fatalistic way of looking at life – what will be will be. It holds out little hope in the use of spontaneous prayer, and it can help produce a hearty dislike of the tiresome enthusiasts who dare to claim some special relationship with God.

In 1781 a local awakening began in the North of England. John Valton and George Snowden had moved to Manchester and were involved in a general revival there. There were many soldiers in camps across the country, because of the wars with France. In 1782, an awakening began among troops stationed near Winchester.

In London, Whitefield's church in Tottenham Court Road was enlarged to seat 5,000, making it the largest Free Church auditorium in the world. There is now a more modern Whitefield Memorial Church on this site.

In the 1740s John Erskine, a minister of the Church of Scotland, published a written 'memorial', seeking to encourage regular prayer in Scotland for an outpouring of the Holy Spirit. He sent it to Jonathan Edwards, a well-known preacher with revival experience, in the America colonies. That inspired Edwards to write his own plea for revival prayer, which Erskine circulated in England in 1794. Among those who received it were two Baptist ministers in Northamptonshire called John Ryland and Andrew Fuller. Back in 1783, John Ryland had baptised a poor shoemaker called William Carey.

Responding to the plea for prayer, many Baptist churches in both Northamptonshire and Leicestershire resolved to hold a prayer meeting for general revival on the first Monday of each month.

Fuller went far and wide telling others about 'The Union of Prayer', which was enthusiastically adopted by Baptists in the Midlands. Other Free Churches joined The Union of Prayer. Methodists recognised their importance and Evangelical Anglicans showed their sympathy. The Union of Prayer became widespread as one denomination after another started having monthly prayer meetings. That paved the way for both revival and an outburst of missionary activity begun by William Carey.

Soon, great numbers were thronging again to the churches and chapels. Baptist church membership in England in the 1790s trebled within 5 years.

Congregationalists caught the flame of revival in the 1790s, and their preachers began to speak with fresh zeal and greater success. William Williams of Wern was a great preacher among the Congregationalists of Wales. Old meeting houses of the denomination became crowded and new ones had to be built.

In 1792-93, Methodist churches in the industrial cities of Yorkshire such as Leeds, Hull and Sheffield experienced a general awakening. Many people were converted through the prayer meetings. Across the Pennines, in the industrial towns of Lancashire, there was a strong move of the Spirit especially under the preaching of Robert Miller.

In 1794 an awakening began in Cornwall. The Cornish people had already been impacted by a controversial preacher called Joseph Benson, who attracted thousands of people to hear him. At Gwenapp, where John Wesley had preached repeatedly, Benson spoke to an audience of 20,000.

Common factors in these awakenings were the role of local evangelists working through established societies, spontaneous gatherings for prayer even at sacrificial hours, and the readiness of local people to attend mass gatherings.

Dissenting (non-Anglican) congregations grew rapidly. In 1700, Dissenters were about 1 in 25 in the English population, whereas a hundred years later they had become about 1 in 4.[1]

In London, the Anglican ministers John Newton and William Romaine founded the Eclectic Society, which proved and remains an effective way of encouraging and sustaining Evangelical clergy within the Anglican Church.

The idea of having 'camp meetings' was imported from America by some Methodists, and a very lively such event was held on the slopes of Mow Cop, north of Stoke-on-Trent, on 31st May 1807. Thousands of Methodists were joined by a considerable number of unconverted people, many of whom came under conviction of sin. Sadly, the annual Methodist Conference in July 1807 rejected the whole idea of camp meetings as both highly improper and liable to lead to trouble.

The main promoter of the camp meetings, Hugh Bourne, was expelled from his local society. He and others continued to pass on new converts to their local societies, but when these people were also rejected they started up their own societies. In 1812, these new societies adopted the name Primitive Methodists, echoing a phrase once used by John Wesley. They soon proved to be more effective at reaching labouring people than the more respectable Wesleyan Methodists.

In 1814, Cornwall was the scene of another revival which started in Redruth and then spread to the rest of the county. People flocked to the chapels, seeking peace with God. The impact was greatest in rural districts, though the towns were also affected. The Methodist circuits experienced a 55% increase of membership in one year.

Anglican Evangelicals remained concerned about the divisive aspects of sending out preachers into other ministers' parishes. A successful strategy adopted by the clergyman Charles Simeon in Cambridge was to help train Evangelical clergy for new churches. By 1815, he was at the height of his influence. His trust, Simeon's Trust, was founded in 1836. It was united as recently as in 1990 with Hyndman's Trust, and the combined trust has nowadays a 'patronage' role in nearly 200 parishes in over 40 dioceses.

The first Evangelical bishop in the Anglican Church was Henry Ryder, made Bishop of Gloucester in 1815. Two Sumner brothers were made bishops, of Winchester and Chester respectively. Beginning in 1827, Anglican Evangelical clergy organised themselves to prepare for coming revival by holding annual Islington Conferences in London.[1, 2]

Revival in Wales

Reports started coming through during the 1780s of local revivals in places like Llangeitho, in what is now Ceredigion, and in both the north and south of Wales. English Baptists and Congregationalists succeeded in interesting Welsh ministers in the Union of Prayer that would pray for revival of God's work at home and abroad.

There was a notable revival in Bala, North Wales, in 1791 under Thomas Charles. Some of the wildest of young people were attracted to it. Some outstanding characters became Christians in awakenings there, including John Elias who went on to be a great preacher.

There were also awakenings in the latter part of the 1700s in Cardigan, Carmarthen, Pembroke, Caernarfon and the Isle of Anglesey. These movements were full of grace and power and did much to raise the moral behaviour of the people. A shoemaker called Christmas Evans was soundly converted in one of these and became one of the ablest preachers in Welsh.

William Williams and Daniel Evans contributed much to the Congregationalists who became the most numerous Free Church in Wales. Further breakthrough was achieved by the Methodists in 1800 after they started to evangelise the Welsh in their own language.

Anglican Evangelical ministers were relatively numerous, but they were not well supported by their bishops until Thomas Burgess was made Bishop of St. David's in 1803. He and other bishops who followed his example managed to bring much greater spirituality into the life of their fellow ministers.

A notable feature of some of the later awakenings in this period was that the Holy Spirit especially impacted children and young people, as first happened in Aberystwyth in 1805.

A move of the Spirit began at Beddgelert, in what is now Gwynedd. A Sunday School teacher successfully urged both young and old to devote their spare time on Sundays to praying for revival. Strong conviction then fell on the whole area, which spread through North Wales and then into South Wales. Many reported hearing what sounded like the massed choirs of heaven singing overhead. The impact of the new converts was felt in the Free Churches in ways proportionate to their previous scale: the Baptists alone gained 8,000 members.

At Bontuchel, in Denbighshire in 1821, an intense revival broke out following the singing of a moving Welsh hymn. The church became fully revived, and the community was so impacted that some previously *hardened* sinners (that is, ones who were considered to be very unlikely to change) were converted.

The awakenings in Wales affected people in both rural and urban areas. In consequence, the working classes were more deeply impacted than in England. The Welsh-speaking ministers worked more closely across the denominations than was ever achieved by their English counterparts. The local chapel typically became the social focus of communities. Singing and hymn writing became a preoccupation of the Welsh people, and the nation first became known as a land of revivals. Another of the special aspects of the awakenings in Wales was the effect it had on the development of Welsh identity and character.

Many Welsh people, including Christians, emigrated to the colonies. Many of those contributed a significant amount to faraway English-speaking communities and congregations.[2]

Revival in Scotland

Scotland has been called a 'land of many revivals'.[3] At this time, in the latter part of the eighteenth century. Christianity was already strongly embedded in the lives and minds of the people of Scotland. Ministers of the 'Moderate' party inside the Church of Scotland provided some determined opposition to revivals. However, the revivals increased the number of enthusiastic candidates for the ministry, which resulted in the multiplication of Evangelical parishes.

The main effectual characters of revival in the four decades from the 1780s onwards were two aristocratic brothers, Robert and James Haldane of Edinburgh. Their effect in Scotland was somewhat comparable to that of the Wesley brothers in England a generation earlier.

The other most notable Scottish preacher in the Church of Scotland was John Macdonald of Ferintosh. He was born on the north coast of Scotland and played such a prominent part in revival, especially in the Highlands, that he has been called the Apostle of the North. He was a versatile, scholarly man, with the ability to preach in English or Gaelic and in the open air.

James Haldane had a first career at sea in the Honourable East India Company. In 1793 he became a ship's captain. He began serving as a non-ministerial evangelist in 1797, which did not endear him to ordained Scottish ministers.

He and a friend were encouraged by previous evidence of interest to go on a preaching tour in 1800 down the peninsula of Kintyre on the west coast, preaching three times a day in the villages. They were arrested at one point but then released, an episode that attracted all the more interest in them by the time they came back up the peninsula. At Campbelltown, at the southern end, they preached to about 1,000 on a Sunday morning and to about 1,500 in the evening. An awakening had begun.

In the same year, James Haldane preached on the Isle of Arran, which then had a population of about 5,000. A slower work of God began there which culminated long after his departure, in 1812, in very fruitful prayer meetings. These were noted for outcries and agitations of both body and mind, followed by the conversion of many.

He and Robert Aikman went on a preaching tour of the North in 1797, preaching in a number of towns between Perth and Aberdeen. He spoke in Thurso, Highland, for some days. The number of people attending at one time reached 3,000. He sent Gaelic speakers to the glens, and their impact was supplemented by the Gaelic preacher John Macdonald.

English evangelicalism had a stimulating effect on Scottish Presbyterians. Whitefield had been very welcome in Scotland. In 1796 Charles Simeon made a visit there in the company of James Haldane. They toured Argyll, Perth and Stirling and were well received. Simeon left a lasting impression, most notably in Perthshire. A 'quiet revival', with no outcries or convulsions, began there that lasted until 1802.

In 1798 the Haldanes invited to Scotland the famous English preacher and pastor Rowland Hill. Hill attracted great crowds wherever he went. In Edinburgh, he spoke to as many as 20,000 at one time. In that same year, Robert and James Haldane founded the Society for the Propagation of the Gospel at Home, in order to employ preachers, circulate literature and establish Sunday schools. By the end of 1799, they had 40 missionaries in the Highlands.

By 1799 the Haldanes and their associates were so unconvinced that renewing change was ever coming in the Presbyterian Church of Scotland that they broke away from it. The outraged Assembly responded by passing rulings against freelancers such as them. However, that never deterred the two brothers from their itinerant ministry, and they helped to establish 85 independent churches across Scotland and Ireland.

In May 1801, the Haldanes' church congregation in Edinburgh moved to a very large new building called the Tabernacle in Leith Walk, and James Haldane was then its minister for nearly 50 years. He preached in many places and the church fed all denominations, which also led to the strengthening of Evangelicals in the established church.

1815, the year of the Battle of Waterloo, was a spiritual turning-point year in Scotland, as it had been elsewhere. Thomas Chalmers became minister of Tron, one of the leading Church of Scotland churches in Glasgow. He gained permission to start a new parish among 10,000 of the city's poorest inhabitants. He divided the parish into 25 sections of 400 people, each with its own elder, deacon and Sunday school teachers. His experiment was a great success, and he preached to huge congregations. Drunkenness and poverty were reduced, and education and morals improved.

Robert Findlater the minister at Ardeonaig, Stirling, invited John MacDonald to share in the work he was doing in the autumn of 1816. 4,000-5,000 people gathered in the open air to hear them, and many conversions were recorded. Findlater described it as 'a universal melting under the word'.[2]

Colonial expansion of the English-speaking world gave Scottish Christians a great opportunity to extend their influence to many places overseas.[2]

Revival in Ireland

Ireland was in a turbulent state at that time, but there was still a comparable awakening there. The circumstances of the French Revolution helped to fuel flames of civil unrest.

The Roman Catholic majority in Ireland were prevented under British law from taking part in various trades and professions, teaching, holding political office, voting or even owning a horse. Some of these inequalities were successfully addressed over this period, but not all. It has been estimated that about only 1 in 500 Catholic households at that time had a Bible, whereas the figure was more like 1 in 3 in Protestant households. Catholics had been oppressed by nominally Protestant rulers for so long that it was a matter of loyalty for many of them to keep to their own form of religion even when revival beckoned.

Despite these discouragements to revival occurring among the Catholic majority, the spiritual tide rose among Methodist churches in the early 1790s. In 1791, at a Methodist meeting place in Newry, County Down, there was a great outpouring of the Spirit and over a hundred conversions were reported. Methodists also became well established in Enniskillen and Ballinamallard.

A rebellion against British rule occurred in Ireland in 1798, which was heavily crushed, causing much local distress to all. In the same year, the Evangelical Society of Ulster was formed for the purpose of extending preaching throughout the province. Its activities helped to further a wish for revival and evangelism.

An Irish counterpart of Charles Simeon arose called Benjamin Williams Matthias, who trained up many young men for the ministry in the Church of Ireland. Some of them later rose to positions of importance. It was not easy for Evangelicals in the Church of Ireland, where sermons were more often moralistic than life-giving. Young clergy such as Peter Roe and Robert Shaw successfully promoted a deepening of spiritual life among the clergy. In protest, a colleague of Shaw's complained to his bishop that Shaw was mad. The bishop replied that if Shaw was mad, he wished he would bite all the clergy in his diocese.

At this time, many Catholics were attracted to attend Protestant churches, sometimes coming over at the rate of hundreds in a month. This brought some persecution on those concerned, which some of them escaped through emigration.

The Methodists had preachers who were bilingual in Gaelic and English. They did evangelism in marketplaces, which exposed them to abuse, dirt and manhandling. Sometimes the open-air preachers gathered a respectful audience of thousands, and at other times their lives were threatened. The work was generally fruitful, and in 1801 alone Methodist membership in Ireland increased by over 25%.

In 1799 an awakening occurred in Bandon in County Cork, where in the space of two weeks about 250 people were converted. People in many places fell to the ground under spiritual conviction. In 1801, the Scottish evangelist James Haldane came to Northern Ireland and preached to great crowds in various towns, including Belfast.

There were not many Baptist churches in Ireland, but these had success in a few places such as Tobermore. Congregational, Moravian and Quaker assemblies also shared in the spiritual prosperity.

A ship's captain, John Newton, left the hardened and godless world of the slave trade as a result of his conversion. He was what may be termed a *trophy of grace*, an example of what the grace of God can do to transform someone who has been a hardened sinner. He remained captain of a slave trading ship after his conversion, but he soon came to realise he should no longer be doing it. He was ordained into the Anglican church and later became vicar of St. Mary Woolnoth in London. He wrote hymns, including the world famous 'Amazing Grace'.[2]

William Wilberforce

William Wilberforce was a dissolute young MP who came spiritually to life in the Great Awakening. He had brilliant powers of speech and was a friend of the highly talented William Pitt, who became Prime Minister of Great Britain in 1801 at the age of 24.

Wilberforce's spiritual direction changed after a reading holiday abroad, during which he had lengthy conversations with his former tutor Dr. Isaac Milner. Wilberforce became thoroughly convinced of the call of God on his life. He went off to John Newton by night to seek his advice about how he should respond to his change of heart. Newton persuaded him to remain a politician and use his talents in Parliament.

Wilberforce was invited by the Committee for the Abolition of the Slave Trade to be their main representative in Parliament. In addition to the aim of abolishing slavery, he also set himself the aim of the reformation of manners. This was not the matter of promoting better public etiquette but about the whole way in which people lived their lives.

For many people, their manner of life lacked much compassion or any readiness to take action on behalf of the poor and vulnerable. Wilberforce's interest in reforming people's manners extended to people's treatment of animals: he was one of the founding members of the RSPCA (the Royal Society for the Protection of Animals).

He remained an Independent MP, never becoming a (political) party man and declining any government appointments offered to them by William Pitt. Wilberforce needed every ally of any party, inside or outside of Parliament, if a vote to abolish slavery could ever be successful. The slave trade was such a mainstay of the British economy and way of doing things that many must have felt that its abolition was beyond the reach of anyone.

It is also possible to learn something from Wilberforce's example. An American visitor who went to see Wilberforce late in his life reported that he found him to be fluent in conversation, modest, remarkably elegant in his way of speaking, careful about forming conclusions, searching with his questions and skillful in weighing people's stories.

Wilberforce wrote a well-received book, *A Practical View of the Prevailing Religious System of Professed Christians*. It explained the Christian faith very well and was read by many: it went into 40 editions and several translations. Many people found faith in Christ through reading it.

The great landmarks of his life were the abolition of the slave trade in 1807 and the abolition of slavery in all British lands and dominions in 1833, which was voted through just a few days before he died on 29th July. 750,000 slaves were set free a year later in the West Indies, without bloodshed. He had retired from Parliament in 1825, leaving the leadership of the anti-slavery movement and other reforms to Sir Thomas Buxton. Back in 1807, when the vote to abolish slavery was successful in Parliament, Wilberforce turned to his friend Henry Thornton MP and asked him what they should abolish next. Thornton's reply was 'the Lottery', which was achieved in 1826.

The Clapham Sect

Wilberforce became involved with others in many other causes, working as part of a group called the Clapham Sect. This exceptional group were intelligent, influential and mainly Anglican campaigners. It all began when Wilberforce and his cousin Henry Thornton moved as bachelors to a house in Clapham in 1782. The two men later married and settled in separate houses, and other friends came to live nearby too. Their families spent much time in each other's homes. In addition to those already related, a number of marriages took place between these likeminded households.

The film *Amazing Grace* (2006) gives a helpful impression of William Wilberforce and some of those who worked with him. The film is focused on the abolition of the slave trade.

Political ability was provided by Henry Thornton (Independent MP for Southwark) who was also the nucleus of the group, William Wilberforce (Independent MP for Yorkshire) and William Smith (Liberal MP for Norwich). Smith was a broadly educated man from one of the dissenting academies, who fought for many freedoms, including freedom of speech and worship.

Legal ability was provided partly by the famous and fiery lawyer James Stephen. Granville Sharp was very proficient at putting together legal arguments. Arguing that English law going back to Magna Carta did not justify slavery, he won a case that freed a slave called James Somerset. Effectively, the Somerset case made slavery illegal in England, with immediate impact on the status of 14,000 black slaves in the country.

Information and evidence was collected by Thomas Clarkson, who at times risked his life from hostile traders. He was a key member of the Committee for the Abolition of the Slave Trade, among whose founding members were 9 Quakers and 3 Anglicans. Zachary Macaulay had encyclopaedic knowledge, so much so that a saying arose in the group "Look it up in Macaulay". Stephen and Macaulay also had direct knowledge and experience of slave plantations.

Experience of high office was also well represented. John Shore (Lord Teignmouth) had once been Governor-General of India. Charles Grant was Chairman and the main director of the East India Company, working from central London. Macaulay was the Governor of Sierra Leone from 1794 to 1799. He helped the colony to improve considerably, and the capital Freetown became a prosperous settlement.

The special quality of Clapham as a relaxing environment and model parish was due mainly to the contributions of John Thornton and then Henry Venn. Thornton bought up the right to appoint clergy in Clapham and beyond. He was then active in the building of a new church, Holy Trinity, on Clapham Common in 1776. Venn became Rector of Clapham in 1793, based in Holy Trinity.

The parish had in it many poor and needy adults and children. Venn transformed Clapham into a mini-welfare state with separate districts. Matters attended to included: the provision of food and clothing, the distribution of blankets, the prevention of epidemics by public health measures, and smallpox vaccination.

How did the group function together in the anti-slavery campaign, apart from holding meetings, sharing information and making resolutions? They tirelessly wrote letters, organised public meetings, uncovered the darker secrets of the slave trade, lobbied people of influence, prayed, invested money in projects, published a regular journal, supported a boycott of sugar and, with their campaigns, helped to support the MPs like Wilberforce in Parliament.

Friends of the group included Equiano, a former slave, and Ignatius Sancho, both of whom gave powerful testimonies as former slaves. Hannah More was an educational reformer and generous giver who wrote plays and poetry. Elizabeth Heyrick was an activist who encouraged the boycott of imported sugar from the West Indies in nearby Leicester. Josiah Wedgewood, the very successful pottery owner, funded the mass production of china cameos with a picture of an African on them, carrying the inscription 'Am I not a Man and a Brother?'

While the abolition of the slave trade was the group's greatest purpose and collective achievement, they did much else in the cause of social reform and the formation of Christian societies. Not all that they attempted was successful, most notably their early attempts to found a colony in Africa for freed slaves. However, they also helped to start the Bible Society, the Church Missionary Society (CMS) and the London Missionary Society. In all, they founded over 20 Christian organisations and societies that supported people and causes such as the poor, orphans, charity schools,

British sailors, the suppression of vice and the protection of girls, widows and elderly single women.[4, 5]

The Methodists as a denomination

It was in this generation that methodism became the Methodist denomination. Ongoing disputes, after Wesley's death, about the status of travelling preachers and the administration of communion ('the sacraments') led to Methodist Conference adopting The Plan of Pacification in 1795. That marked a decisive break from the Church of England. In the generation after John Wesley's death, Methodist numbers grew from about 71,000 to almost a quarter of a million.

Separation from the Anglicans brought about the need to start building chapels. Some of this could be very costly for those taking part. The local clergyman might be very unhappy to see some of his former congregation setting up a rival meeting place of worship. If he was in close working relationship with the local landowner, some labourers lost their jobs and, therefore, their home as part of the cost of being a Methodist.

A critical and telling impression of early local Methodists has been left by the Anglican clergyman and diarist John Skinner, who was Rector in the Somerset village of Camerton from 1800 to 1839. I have had the interest of visiting his parish and church. In his journals recording all the main events of his life and ministry, he can be seen to fit well with the description already given of deism. He was a well-educated, generous and cultured man, but he was most antagonistic towards the Methodists in his parish, for instance expressing his outrage at their claims of ministering deathbed conversions.

The beginnings of the Brethren

Another Christian movement that came into being in that fruitful era was the Brethren. This began as the Assembly Movement in Ireland in the 1820s. Dr. Edward Cronin, a dentist in Dublin, was a former Roman Catholic who professed an evangelical conversion. He then found himself expected to choose to belong to just one of several Protestant denominations. He and other likeminded people of influence became unhappy with denominationalism, and this made them want to unite believers in a restoration of New Testament Christianity. This could be said to spring from a sincere wish to be known as a Christian and no more than that.

J.N. Darby, a forceful and brilliant Anglican curate, became the main leader of the Movement. In England they were known as the Christian Brethren or as the Plymouth Brethren. In Bristol, George Müller became famous for his Homes for Orphans, as well as having oversight of the Brethren Assembly of Bethesda. There was a parting of the ways from J.N. Darby after Bethesda received relocated members from an assembly in Plymouth that Darby had excluded. Other leaders like A.N. Groves sided with Müller.

In 1848, those that followed Müller became known as the *Open Brethren*, maintaining some level of open fellowship with other Christians, while those more exclusively following Darby were called the *Exclusive Brethren*. The

Brethren became notable for their devotion to prayer and studying and teaching the Bible, which helps to show how it was that the movement became a proving ground for a number of future church leaders.[6]

The Age of Reason

Besides the Great Awakening, another way of thinking arising at that time was 'the Age of Reason', or the Enlightenment. The main proponents of that were people like the political theorist and activist Thomas Paine, who championed reason and free thought. The influence of the Enlightenment continues strongly in the UK to this day.

Some consequences on society and the world

Some of the greatest consequences from this era were:

- ☑ The abolition of the slave trade and then of slavery itself in the United Kingdom and its dominions. The Royal Navy set up a West Africa Squadron to help suppress the whole of the slave trade there.
- ☑ Support created for the vulnerable and for victims of slavery
- ☑ The lifting of morals in UK society generally, including added protection of women and children
- ☑ Development of the Welsh identity, including their love of music and singing. Wales has been called the 'land of song'. A speaker promoting Welsh identity, especially but not only its rugby, communicates with a selfless passion that is evocative of a revival.

☑ Impacts on the whole English-speaking world, in both community and church life, as many capable Christians emigrated.

Thought for Reflection

William Wilberforce and the rest of the Clapham Sect produced a great team effect that went far beyond the considerable talents of its individual members.

Prayer

Lord, what further teams can be formed today that can bring together such different Christian talents as were seen in the Clapham Sect?

4

Later descendants of the Evangelical Awakening

Their only suggestion was that we keep on helping the poor, which I have always been eager to do.

(Galatians 2:10)

The generation of Evangelicals who were active from 1830 to 1860 can be described as the grandchildren of the Great Awakening. This conveys the thought that there was a new generation still working out the revelations and writings left by great predecessors like the Wesleys. The social impact of what was achieved was enormous. There are writers today suggesting that we have reached the end of Capitalism. In fact, there were reasons for very low confidence in Capitalism at the time of this chapter. It was a time when some of the worst excesses of the Agricultural and Industrial Revolutions were courageously confronted by both rich and poor Christians. The lives of millions of British people, especially among the working class, were affected in some way for the better by the changes achieved.[1]

Revivals were happening locally at this time, but they became less common from soon after 1850. God was nonetheless at work preparing a new generation of leaders, like the young Charles Haddon Spurgeon and William Booth, to be in their spiritual prime in time for the next wave of revival that would come in 1859.

How local revivals developed across the country: Waterloo and beyond

Anxious days before the Battle of Waterloo in 1815 helped to create conditions in which many turned to God in prayer. In Salisbury, an outpouring of the Spirit occurred two months before Waterloo, which was preceded by and led to much prayer. At the end of April, 1,000 people were crowded into the Methodist Chapel there (now called Salisbury Methodist Church). The move of God overflowed to nearby villages like Wilton. Revival continued for a year, including reaching the nearby town of f.

The Primitive Methodists under the leadership of Hugh Bourne continued to thrive. He noted that Wesley had approved women preachers as well as open-air preaching. Sarah Kirkland was one whose preaching was well received. In 1816 she helped to lead a camp meeting in woodland near Nottingham, attended by 1,200 people. That event was the start of a widespread awakening in the Midlands, which greatly increased the Primitive Methodist following. The denomination held its first Connexional Conference in 1820.

Another Methodist offshoot was the Bible Christians, who began in Devon in 1815. They reached other parts of England and flourished mostly in Cornwall. They claimed to have a more evangelistic thrust than the Wesleyan Methodists. Their leaders included a memorable, frank-speaking character called Billy Bray, who was called 'the apostle of joy'.

In 1821, reports of revival were widespread, including in Kent and Lancashire and in Leeds, Liverpool, Banbury, Sunderland, Maidstone, Derby, Tenterden, Newcastle-under-Lyme, and in the cathedral cities of Canterbury and Durham.

Despite the appearance of the new groups claiming to be more like Wesley than the Wesleyan Methodists, and continuing to expand, the central Methodist denomination grew steadily and reached a quarter of a million by the 1830s.

Another Union of Prayer was started up in 1823 in several large cities and towns. One of the characteristics of these prayer meetings was the genuineness of their union, drawing together Free Church ministers and Evangelical Anglicans to deliver courses of lectures. Revivals were reported in various places. In fact, talk of revivals had become so commonplace that it became more customary to refer to the prosperity of the work rather than to revival.

The Congregationalist churches began to change in response to the awakening occurring in the country. They became less focused on teaching exactitude and more on evangelism. The demand for ministers came to exceed the supply.

The Baptists were influenced in a similar way. In the first three decades of the nineteenth century they doubled their number of members and churches. Robert Hall attracted many highly educated people with his eloquence.

Within those same three decades, most Presbyterians had become Unitarians. Other Presbyterian congregations stayed on as they were, and others joined the Congregational churches.

Evangelicals across the denominations came to have more central influence, due to their growing numbers and their level of confidence. It was partly due to the increasing Christian impact on the social fabric of the nation, where former plantation slaves were now freed and better laws and conditions were won for those working amid the harsh conditions and brutalities of the Agricultural and Industrial Revolutions.[2]

The 1830s

There was another series of local revivals among the Methodist churches in England. In 1834 in Yeadon, in Yorkshire, a revival so affected the town that normal business stopped in some houses for several days. The revival spread to nearby places. The 600 members of the local chapel welcomed 900 new converts.

Wesleyan Methodist societies had another revival in the early 1840s, as an overflow of American Methodism. James Caughey was an Irish-born emigrant to the United States, who felt a call to return to the British Isles for evangelism. He first spoke in Dublin and then Liverpool, where he preached a total of 120 times and saw more than 1,200 converts added to the churches.

In Nottingham, the new converts included a young man called William Booth, who then took to street preaching. Caughey continued his very successful tour and reaped a spiritual harvest in Huddersfield, Goole, Sheffield, York, Chesterfield and Birmingham. Sometimes he reached Baptists and Congregationalists as well as Methodists. In total, he claimed his preaching led to 22,000 converts.

Over time, the diligent Wesleyan Methodists moved up the social scale and became more respectable, showing rather less interest in evangelism and revival in the process. Meanwhile, the smaller Methodist denominations like the Primitive Methodists, the New Connexion, the Bible Christians and others continued their outreach among the masses.

The pattern of revival in Wales in the 1830s and 1840s was that of sporadic awakenings, sometimes affecting one county or maybe all of North Wales or all of South Wales. The Free Churches were the ones who gained the most members in the process. By the mid-1800s, Wales had become a nation of chapels.

This was a traumatic time in Ireland's history, because of disease and famine. While some people in England were leaving Protestantism for the Church of Rome, the opposite was happening in Ireland as many Catholics joined the Free Churches. This era in Ireland has been called the 'second Reformation'.

In 1832, Ireland was hit by a cholera epidemic which killed thousands. Many Irish people became religiously interested at that time, and not a few emigrated to avoid persecution for doing so. During the early 1830s, the number of Wesleyan Methodists increased by 4,000. The Presbyterians built a hundred new churches in the 1830s.

In the early 1830s, there was the rise of a movement in the Church of Scotland that would have far-reaching importance, arising from their resistance to the continuation of *lay patronage* where clergy appointments were made by local landowners rather than by the church. In 1834, the General Assembly of the church agreed to raise funds for 200 more churches and to support a right of veto over whoever had been appointed by landowners.

The prominent Scottish leaders of that time were notable ministers such as John, Horatius and Andrew Bonar, Robert Murray McCheyne in Dundee, Thomas Chalmers in Glasgow, W.H. Burns in Kilsyth (near Glasgow), John Macdonald in Inverness and John Milne in Perth. Opposition to revival came from the declining party of Moderates within the Church of Scotland.

Another contributing factor leading to a resurgence in Anglican church attendance in those decades, though not strictly a revival in the terms defined in this book, was the Oxford Movement. It was certainly a religious revival. As a result of starting to publish its own 'tracts' from 1833 onwards, this movement also became known as the Tractarian Movement, with the clergyman John Keble as one of its main leaders. This scholarly, High Church movement stressed rebirth through infant baptism, spiritual devotion through the celebration of the sacraments (communion) and a recovery of traditional forms and customs of pre-Reformation England. While both Tractarians and Evangelicals attained a new level of church life in these decades, and together helped to add a new level of vigour to the Church of England, they did not see eye to eye and indeed had very different priorities.

Some Tractarians were so much in favour of Catholic ways that they later left the Anglican church for the church of Rome, the most outstanding of them being John Newman who was later made a Cardinal. Two of William Wilberforce's sons became Tractarians and later became Catholics, while a third remained a loyal Evangelical and later became Bishop of Winchester.

With so many more people attending on Sundays, the Anglican church began a new programme of church building. Five hundred more churches were built by 1830 and three times that number in the 1840s, due especially to the work of the Church Building Society. Extensions and galleries were added to many existing structures. Sunday church attendance became more of a respectable and typical feature of life, as can be seen in the literature and in films that portray that time.

A public holiday was given for 20th June 1837, the day of the coronation of Queen Victoria. George Moberly, the devout headmaster of Winchester College and close friend of John Keble, was sorry to miss so much of the celebrations on that happy day because of having to attend yet another meeting of the Church Building Society. He observed how the people of Winchester were moved at the thought of having such a young queen come to the throne.

The various spiritual qualities of Victoria's long reign from that day onwards were due in considerable measure to the influence of the godly man she later married, Prince Albert of Saxe-Coburg. Yet another German influence would benefit the spiritual life of the nation. Partly inspired by Lord Shaftesbury, Prince Albert was the first person in the Royal Family to show a deep interest in social welfare, which continues prominently in the Royal Family to this day.

In the summer of 1839 in Kilsyth, William Chalmers Burns, who was the son of W.H. Burns already mentioned, organised some special meetings. The church already had a high level of prayer and a great interest in foreign missions. He preached on the text 'Thy people shall be willing in the day of Thy power' (Psalm 110:3). As he told the congregation about the great work of God at the Kirk of Shotts in 1630, he felt so moved that he began to plead with them for an immediate response. The large audience broke from usual restraint so strongly that their crying and praying drowned him out. Some screamed and others fell to the ground.

Following that occasion, the churches of the town worked so well together that between 12,000 and 15,000 locals and visitors joined their special services on 22nd September. The services were held all day and some lasted until daybreak on the Monday. Multitudes professed conversion. The spiritual and moral condition of the town began to change. Every street had a prayer meeting and there were nightly sermons.[3]

W.C. Burns preached at St. Peter's, Dundee (now called St. Peter's Free Church) while the church's minister Robert Murray McCheyne was away in the second half of 1839. McCheyne was in Palestine for six months with Andrew Bonar. A work of conviction among the 1,000-strong congregation in St. Peter's, well prepared by the ministry of McCheyne, broke out like a pent-up flood. McCheyne heard about the revival in Hamburg on his return journey. He gladly continued the work on his return. The church had held 39 prayer meetings by November 1839, and by that date more than 700 enquirers had been instructed in the faith. Afterwards he said, 'The number of saved souls is far beyond my knowledge'. The revival then spread to some local places such as Collace.[4, 5]

In Perth, John Milne welcomed Burns in 1839 to St. Leonard's Church (now St. Leonard's in the Fields, in Marshall Place). Shortly after Burns' arrival, a revival began in late December and went on for three months. There were two meetings in the daytime and there were packed nightly meetings. The congregation soon grew to over 800 members.

From Perth, Burns started making evangelistic journeys across Perthshire and Fife and then to Aberdeen and beyond. Many of the reports of his preaching mentioned his emphasis on the love of Christ in dying for sinners, though most conversions occurred during seasons of prayer rather than directly after hearing his preaching.

He was invited by Duguld Campbell to the village of Lawers, near Loch Tay. At least 3,000 gathered to hear him on 23rd August 1840. Typically respectable listeners were awakened at a moral level. Many of his listeners had floods of tears coming down their cheeks as they became convinced of the evil of sin and the sinner's need for a hiding place from the storm. Following that, he kept up a very busy preaching schedule and covered great distances on horseback in fulfilment of his many engagements.[3]

The 1840s

In 1840, more than 2,000 were added to the churches in a move of God affecting North Wales, Liverpool and parts of

South Wales. Those promoting the work had been studying the lectures on revival given recently by Charles Finney in the United States, so they followed a pattern of arranging prayer meetings and then organising district evangelism.

In the winter of 1841-42 there was a great revival in Leith, the port of Edinburgh. The pattern was the usual one: much prayer beforehand, great expectations of revival, a deep conviction of sin, genuine repentance, followed by transformation of character.

In the Borders, Horatius Bonar reported more than 100 conversions in Kelso where he was the minister. An awakening was also reported in Jedburgh. The revival then spread south-west to Annan, on the north side of the Solway Firth. All over the Lowlands of Scotland, great crowds of people attended the churches.

In the Western Highlands, there was there a great awakening in Oban, in Argyllshire, causing people to flock into the town from miles around. Another work of grace began in 1843 in the nearby island of Lismore, in the Inner Hebrides.

Resistance to lay patronage came to a head at the General Assembly of the Church of Scotland in 1842. The Assembly declared by a large majority that the civil courts had jurisdiction in civil cases but no right to interfere with the government and discipline of the church. The Prime Minister Robert Peel persuaded Parliament in Westminster to reject this appeal for change. In response, Robert Chalmers and about 450 other ministers left the Church of Scotland in 1843, which meant giving up their churches and their homes. Following this 'Disruption' many of them, though not all, reconvened to form the evangelical Free of Church of Scotland. Some of them joined and strengthened other denominations like the Baptists.

The Church of Scotland was left with 729 ministers, down to nearly 60% of its former number. Some large churches in Edinburgh were left almost empty. However, the Church of Scotland recovered. It abolished lay patronage 30 years later.

The Highlands largely went over to the Free Church. The Free Church built more than 600 churches in the next few years. It founded New College in Edinburgh and maintained all the overseas missionaries.

In 1845, blight affected the Irish potato crop, and the following year the potato crop failed completely. Widespread famine was the result. Here was another kind of major trauma. Large numbers died and many more were forced to emigrate, especially to the United States. There was nonetheless such a hunger for God in those years that Methodist churches gained as many people as the Methodists who emigrated. There were local revivals in several parts of the North of Ireland in the years following the famine.

In 1849, a 17-year-old called James Hudson Taylor, later to become one of the country's greatest ever missionaries, had first-hand experience of a time of great spiritual blessing during his first few months as a Christian. God moved powerfully in a mission in his church led by Dr Greenbury, which was Pitt Street Chapel in Barnsley. In four evenings, about 100 people were in his words 'taken who had found peace'. Hudson Taylor helped to take down some names and talked to some of the many enquirers. He commented, 'Oh, we had a gracious time of it!'[6]

In 1849 there was also a great cholera epidemic affected South Wales, which could be seen as another parallel with the coronavirus pandemic which broke out in 2020. The epidemic caused concern among thousands and led to such a sudden increase in church membership that there were concerns that many of the new members would later fall away from the faith. In general, those fears were not realised. The 67 Congregationalist churches across Monmouth, Glamorgan, Brecknock and Carmarthenshire received over 9,000 converts at that time.

In 1850, moves of God happened in some of the Scottish islands, including Skye, Tiree, Mull and Bute. In the Northern Highlands, the Gaelic-speaking John MacDonald preached in towns such as Tain. His Bible-based preaching led to a tide of feeling in the congregation, resulting in the sound of crying coming from every part of the densely crowded congregation.

Many Scots emigrated overseas at this time, and their experience of revivals made their contribution to churches and education overseas an evangelical one.[3]

The Tolpuddle Martyrs

Harsh social conditions were not confined to life in the towns and cities. Six agricultural labourers from Tolpuddle in Dorset are remembered by this name, three of whom were Methodist preachers while two others were Methodist church members. The sixth one became a Christian, and a

Sunday School Superintendent in later life, following their unjust experiences.

A serious legal injustice came down on the heads of these six men in 1834 involving an unjust conviction, which was followed by their deportation to Australia. Tolpuddle is not that far from the home of Thomas Hardy, though the nature of these men's tribulations did not receive any mention in his novels about rural life in 'Wessex'.

One of the six men was a preacher called George Loveless, and his leadership skills and experience of public speaking enabled him to become their spokesman. He was one of the first former Methodist preachers in the country to give working people a public voice on behalf of the poor. The story illustrates that some who helped to stimulate social reform were not the titled or rich but were labouring people who were in some measure the fruit of the recent waves of revival that had been sweeping the country.

Agricultural wages were typically very low at that time. These men were paid little money and they were allowed only slight access to the produce of the farm where they laboured. They were allowed to bring home a loaf of wheaten bread once a week, but otherwise their staple food was barley bannocks and maize junkets. In other words, their pay and conditions as farm labourers did not even allow them ordinary daily bread.

The men were encouraged by a visiting Trade Secretary to form a little agricultural Union together and ask the landowner jointly for a pay rise. Their visitor advised them to keep their Union a secret. That agreement was not essential to their cause, but it was later used decisively against them in court. The landowner Squire Frampton was asked by them to give his workers a pay rise from 7 shillings a week to 10 shillings, which was not a great improvement but would have been enough to lift them off from the partial starvation they were then experiencing on their wages.

The six men were thrown into jail in Dorchester for daring to ask for a pay rise. Judge Baron Williams was sent to try the case, and it is apparent that he had been chosen and briefed in London to make a harsh example of them.

The men were found guilty of having made a secret oath, a highly debatable crime at a time when rich people might belong to a secret society themselves. The six men were sentenced to deportation to Australia for seven years. In consequence of the ruling, the men's households were evicted from their tied accommodation by Squire Frampton. One of the six was not even part of the group, but did the very Christ-like thing of not speaking up about his wrongful arrest in order to save his married brother from being taken away with the rest of the group in custody.

A hue and cry was set up nationally in support of the six men. Thomas Wakely MP was their greatest champion in Parliament, and William Cobbett the pamphleteer supported their cause. 30,000 workers marched in London on their behalf, in the first Trades Union demonstration ever seen. It was led by Arthur Wade who was there in his full academic regalia, as chaplain to the Metropolitan Trade Unions. It was an interesting symbolism of the church leading the Union's cause for justice.

No campaigning efforts were made by the Methodist Church against the court's ruling, consistent with their founder John Wesley who would not have approved of any Methodist campaigns to resist court decisions. However, an aroused level of public opinion finally resulted in the men being given a free pardon and restitution.

Once back in England, the men were paid enough compensation that they and their families could set up farms of their own elsewhere. Only one of them finally settled down in Tolpuddle. The men's pioneering stand for what might now be called a living wage, and their later vindication, paved the way for better wages for those working in agriculture.[7]

Lord Shaftesbury

Anthony Ashley Cooper was known as Lord Ashley from the age of 10 until he became the 7th Earl of Shaftesbury when he was 50. He is generally remembered as Lord Shaftesbury. He and William Wilberforce were the greatest Christian legislators of the nineteenth century. They were both independents politically, rather than party men.

Despite the wealth and social position of Ashley Cooper's parents, he was seriously neglected as a child. An old servant of the household called Maria Miller was a godsend to him and became his spiritual mother, though she died when he was just eight years old.

A formative incident happened in front of Ashley when he was 14 years old, deeply affecting the direction of his life. He witnessed the rude songs of drunken funeral bearers in a street in Harrow, while he was at school there. In their drunken stupor, the casket bearers all fell over while trying to turn together at a street corner and they dropped the casket. The degradation of this incident at a pauper's funeral made Ashley Cooper pray quietly on the spot. It subsequently motivated him to dedicate his life to the downtrodden and the oppressed. There is a plaque close to the place in Harrow where this event happened.

Ten years later, a comparable incident, though not directly witnessed by him, was the death of his younger brother in a fight with another boy at Eton. The boy who had caused the injuries was acquitted because both of them had been given so much brandy between the rounds of their open fight.

Ashley Cooper first became an MP in 1826, when he was in his mid-twenties. He was a very honourable and honest man. As an illustration of this, he said the following memorable words in the parliamentary debate of the Ten Hours Factory Bill in 1844, "Whatever is morally right can never be politically wrong, and whatever is morally wrong can never be politically right."

He was a deeply practical man. In one of his many speeches, he said "Christianity as applied is absolutely and essentially practical." He despised materialism and saw the physical world as a neutral power that could be used for good or ill according to the nature of the ideals controlling it. The spiritual world was, to him, the place in which all true aspirations are born. Therefore, great faith must come before great work.

His approach to the marvels of scientific development was both very positive and guarded. He welcomed and encouraged all that science and engineering might achieve and make possible, but he argued that these developments have both constructive and destructive potential. Society must, therefore, exercise its responsibility to examine very carefully all claims to new aspects of truth.

He called himself an 'evangelical of evangelicals', which reflected his loyalty to all those of an evangelical (Bible-believing) persuasion, not just the members of one denomination. As a result of the huge number of chapel foundation stones he laid in the UK, it was joked that future people digging up the land would conclude he must have been a king.

Shaftesbury's contribution was supremely to help bring in legislation at Westminster that upheld the rights of the poor and the vulnerable. He said it was shameful to the nation that some of this legislation was ever needed, because the humanity and common sense of some employers had been so lacking.

He had a high view of the influential role of women in society. The legislation that he introduced reflected his emphasis on the welfare of women, young people and children. He removed children from working in factories, mines and other dangerous forms of labour. He promoted the education of children. Laws that he introduced also safeguarded women in the workplace. The laws limited the number of hours that people could work in factories, given the dangers of tiredness associated with operational machines.

Shaftesbury also prevented workers from being deprived of their evenings and Sunday leisure. His legislation even made possible for workers to have a Saturday afternoon for sport and recreation. Not content with that, he did much to promote activities that people could do in the spare time that he had won for them.

He promoted the education of children, with character building as its primary purpose. He believed that a nation's best defence lay in the integrity of its citizens. He strongly opposed those who maintained that the best way to manage the masses was to keep them ignorant. He thought the opposite, that uneducated voters could be like a suicidal sword in the hands of the many, or could be a happy hunting ground for those who could appeal to people's basic and selfish instincts.

As early as 1854, Lord John Russell praised Shaftesbury for having done more than anyone else alive to promote the welfare of the working classes. At Shaftesbury's death in 1885, a *1d* (that is, one old penny) subscription was set up to help create a lasting memorial to him. Many people across the world know of this memorial in London without having realised what it really is or who contributed to it. The idea of the *1d* subscription was that any working person could afford to have a part in the memorial. The metalwork was made with the melted-down hoard of the pennies given.

The memorial is a fountain, symbolic of life and yet also helpful to the poor. Rising above the fountain is a statue of Christian love, the self-giving kind of love that this political reformer had shown so strongly. The sculptor intended a pun on Shaftesbury's name as the angelic Eros-like figure fires its 'shaft' into the Empire. Many people mistakenly think that the statue depicts romantic love. The Shaftesbury memorial, misnamed as the Statue of Eros even in guide books, is located at Piccadilly Circus. It is actually a powerful expression of poor people's gratitude to Lord Shaftesbury and his self-giving love for them. It seems very appropriate that a new road being built nearby through an area of former terrible slums was named Shaftesbury Avenue.[8, 9]

Prison reform was another area of British social reforms by evangelicals who were directly or indirectly inspired by recent revivals. John Howard gave his life and his fortune in beginning the process of prison reform. Elizabeth Fry, a Quaker mother of 11 children, regularly went into prisons and founded a society for prison reform in 1817. Their reforms successfully introduced changes such as separation of the sexes, the classification of criminals, useful forms of employment, education and religious instruction for prisoners.

A German visitor called Theodor Fliedner came over to England and visited these and other works. He noticed the reforming methods were all being done by Christians, and he was thoroughly won to their causes and beliefs. On returning to Germany, he set up works for ex-prisoners, orphans, the sick and the insane at Kaiserwerth on the Rhine.

An English gentlewoman Florence Nightingale was intrigued to hear of Fliedner's new works, where German deaconesses from a peasant background took such good care of the people. In those days, no British gentlewoman would get involved in such practical work, but Florence Nightingale went over to Germany and learned how to nurse.[9]

By the time of her death in her 90s, this one believing woman had helped to revolutionise the life and health of the British soldier. She has had a greater impact on nursing generally than anyone else in history, so it was altogether fitting that her name was used for a number of newly opened NHS hospitals during the coronavirus pandemic.

Some consequences for society and the world

- ☑ Slaves were set free in all British dominions following their emancipation by Act of Parliament in 1833.
- ☑ The raw capitalism exposed in the Agricultural and Industrial Revolutions was significantly tamed by the introduction of many laws.
- ☑ British trade unionism developed in strength to stand up for the concerns of labourers as a result of the courage and steadfastness of the Tolpuddle Martyrs.
- ☑ The changes and liberties brought about by Christians in these decades were very important in helping to forge some aspects of the character of the British people of today.

Thought for Reflection

All those *1d* contributions from working people to Lord Shaftesbury's memorial at Piccadilly Circus are a powerful testimony to the lasting impact he had on so many lives.

Prayer

Lord, please guide us to find and pioneer new ways to help the poor in our generation.

5

The 1859 Revival

After these things I heard something like a loud voice of a great multitude in heaven, saying, "Hallelujah! Salvation and glory and power belong to our God".

(Revelation 19:1, NASV)

This is the least widely recorded major revival in the history of the UK, although it was one of the biggest and most widespread. It has also been called 'a people's revival', 'the international revival', 'the forgotten revival' or simply 'The Ulster Revival'. The expression 'the Second Evangelical Awakening' was used by Edwin Orr, who has produced one of the most thorough studies of it.[1] Tony Cauchi calls it 'the Fourth Great Awakening of 1857 Onwards', having distinguished a second one of 1792 onwards and a third of 1830 onwards.[2]

From the outset, there was little disunity between the Protestant denominations, and many joint meetings were held. If there was any serious disunity, it was inside some denominations. The revival flourished best among denominations that encouraged every member to have a ministry and which could most readily enable their most articulate recent converts to share their experiences.

The involvement of volunteers ('laymen') was crucial from the beginning. Inter-denominational prayer meetings were another notable feature. In a number of places, children were touched by God before their parents were.

Outside Ulster, there were relatively few examples of manifestations that could disturb sensitive onlookers or the press, and even then these did not stir up much trouble. God raised up some preachers with very different class backgrounds, sometimes sharing the same platform, who were able to reach those people in their audiences most like themselves. Some of the memorable preachers were *trophies of grace*, fascinating individuals to listen to, whose unrighteous lives had been turned the right way round by their recent repentance and new-found life in Christ.

Revival in a given place took on a typical shape and order: (1) the setting up of prayer meetings for revival; (2) planned evangelism in the area; (3) work to bring about social improvements.[1]

Origins of the revival

The origins of the revival can be traced overseas to both Hamilton, Ontario (in Canada), and New York.

A move of God happened amongst the Methodists of Hamilton, Ontario, in 1857. 300-400 people were saved in the space of a few days. All sectors of society were affected right up to the Mayor of the city. The leadership of these events was in the hands of lay (non-professional) church members.

A report of the events in Hamilton featured in a periodical called the *Christian Advocate*, and was read with eagerness by pastors of the Methodist Episcopal Church across North America. Revivals can be highly infectious, and in the following months reports came to the magazine of small awakenings happening in various states across America. By the late winter of 1858, reports of local revivals had become a flood.

Meanwhile on the 1st July 1857, a newly appointed city missionary, Jeremiah Lanphier, of the Dutch Reformed Church in downtown New York advertised a noon-time prayer meeting in order to help reach the floating population of the area. At the advertised time, no-one had arrived. Then, at 12:30pm one person came, and then four more. On the following Wednesday, 20 people were present. 40 people came the next week. In the first week of October, it was decided to hold the meetings daily. It was in that same week that the revival occurred in Hamilton in Canada. In the second week of October there was a great financial crash, affecting business everywhere. Within 6 months, 10,000 New York businessmen were meeting for prayer. Within two years, 1,000,000 converts had been added to American churches.[3]

Revival in Ireland

Given all the American connections with Ireland, it is not surprising that the revival first reached the United Kingdom in Ulster. Reports of revival in America were already in every major newspaper in the United States. Hearing of it, the General Assembly of the Presbyterian Church in Ireland sent two members to go and report back. The two men were thrilled by what they saw. Reports given in Ulster led to many sermons being preached and prayer meetings for revival held. The revival preparation made was as inter-denominational as the outbreak of the Holy Spirit that followed.

The Ulster Revival was received with great feeling by the common people and resulted in very moving meetings being held, often with spiritual manifestations occurring such as people being so deeply convicted about their sins that they were unable to remain standing.

The first evidence of the revival happened in connection with a prayer meeting that had been started a year earlier by a newly converted young man called James McQuilkin in the village of Kells near Ballymena. A convert of this group, called Samuel Campbell, went back home at Christmas time to his village of Ahoghill, keen to share what had happened to him. His mother and sister turned to God overnight. His brother also professed faith later, after three weeks of strong conviction of his sins. Campbell went back home on another visit and shared everything with a related family, leading to a stirring of interest in the whole neighbourhood.

James McQuilkin, the prayer meeting leader, then took two of his original group to Ahoghill and was allowed to lead a meeting on 2nd February 1859 in the First Presbyterian Church there. Some believed and some mocked, with some criticism expressed about 'lay preachers'. The three young men made a repeat visit a fortnight later, and prayer meetings then multiplied. However, so many people came to a further meeting at the church on 14th March that it was thought prudent just to dismiss them all for reasons of safety. A layman then spontaneously addressed the crowd of about 3,000 in the chilling rain. Hundreds of people fell to their knees in the mud, and many were prostrated in conviction of sin. David Adams the minister there later said that 700 people had been converted.

The depth of feeling felt by many during the Ulster Revival was due to the serious conviction of sin that spontaneously affected unsaved people. A consciousness of their own sinfulness, sometimes accompanied by vivid recollections of regrettable deeds done long ago, and verses taught in childhood, all crowded into their thoughts. The combined effect was strong enough to cause many of these sufferers to be *prostrated*, that is they cried out and fell to the ground under the weight of their agonised feelings. Their sense of pain could go on for minutes, hours or days. Many needed individual ministry to help them to understand how the Saviour had died to carry away all their sins.

Some of the most amazing effects of the revival happened to boys and girls. This was most strongly seen in two schools. At a boys school in Coleraine, one of the boys became distressed enough by conviction of sin that his teacher sent him home with a converted boy. On the way home, they stopped to pray. The troubled boy was then so flooded with God's peace that he said that he wanted to go back to the school and tell his teacher about it.

On arrival back at the school, the boy told his teacher, "I am so happy: I have the Lord Jesus in my heart!" The class were listening as he spoke. One by one they slipped off to be alone in the playground, and when their teacher saw them all kneeling in prayer out there he asked the converted boy to go and comfort them. Soon, the whole school was in a strange state of disorder. Clergy were sent for, who then spent many hours counselling schoolboys, parents, teachers, schoolgirls and neighbours. The ministry did not finish until 11pm in the evening.

Another outbreak happened at a girls school in Armagh. A boy arrived in a breathless state to ask a nearby Presbyterian minister to come quickly to the school. Without having had any Bible teaching beforehand, the girls were 'crying out for mercy'.[4] This happened at a time when there was great interest in the city about the revival.

Prominent effects were witnessed in Belfast and Dublin. Both cities had a large proportion of Protestants, who were generally more open than most Roman Catholics to revival. As these were large cities, they attracted many interested visitors when the press reported that revival was happening. Some ships travelling in and out from Dublin became the place of prayer meetings and there were conversions of passengers and crew. One of the student converts in Dublin, Robert Anderson, went on in later life to be Assistant Commissioner of the Metropolitan Police in London.

Prayer meetings and mass meetings were a common feature as the revival spread. It was usual for a prayer meeting to include an introductory message, sometimes from a visiting speaker. Mass meetings were held out in the fields, especially when clergy were working together. Attendances at the mass meetings were sometimes countable in thousands, and the number of local conversions was often countable in hundreds.

An important factor affecting attendances and responses was the view of the revival taken by the local ministers. If they were all in agreement, especially including the clergy from the Church of Ireland, then the acceptance of the revival in a community was all the greater.

The Press made their own contribution. A Belfast paper picked up early on the story of the revival's beginnings in Ballymena. It reported favourably at first but, as the revival spread across Ireland, it became a fierce critic. Bad publicity can still become useful publicity at times of revival.

Effects on the converted resulted in much higher church attendances, higher Sunday school attendances, greater honesty, and reductions of drunkenness, sexual immorality and swearing. In some cases, as happened in Coleraine, the local courts had practically no-one to try for any criminal offence. Some church buildings had to be extended to seat the larger number of people now coming regularly.

There was almost a complete absence of provocative marching by Orangemen during the revival, and some local public figures noted the softening effect of the revival on the community. The added strength of Christianity in Ulster resulting from this revival is still felt to this day.

The revival spilled over in due course into the other provinces of Ireland. Its spread, mostly where Protestants were already well established, was much longer in taking hold than in Ulster.[4]

Revival in Wales

Its beginning was unconnected with the Ulster Revival. A young Welsh preacher in America, called Humphrey Jones, felt led by God to return to Wales in the summer of 1858. He preached with some success in Wesleyan Methodist chapels, which brought him to the attention of a local minister called David Morgan, who had been praying for ten years for an outpouring of the Divine Spirit. He went reluctantly to hear Jones speak in a Methodist chapel in Ysbyty Ystwyth, unreadily because he distrusted anything coming from America or Wesleyan Methodism. He was nonetheless deeply convicted about the lukewarm state of his own faith, and he entered into an experience of spiritual deepening a few days later.

Morgan shared ministry with Jones for a few months, and he went on to become a significant man in the revival. Based in a village of 1,000 people, he helped to lead 200 of them to the faith by the end of 1858. He started visiting other villages from the start of the new year. The Calvinistic Methodists gained the greatest numbers in the following months, with 9,000 new converts by the summer. The whole county of Cardiganshire became filled with lively religious feeling. Morgan later compared the outbreak of the revival to the touch of an electric switch that detonated a quarry explosion into a thousand hurling pieces.

One of the stories told from that time is about a believing couple in the village of Pontrhydfendigaid, where their wayward son William who was a collier had left them for a wasteful way of living at some unknown address in a 'far country' (actually Glamorgan). They prayed earnestly for

William, and he then happened to arrive back home on the very day when David Morgan was speaking that evening in the nearby chapel. William's first words were to ask if everything was alright. Three days earlier he had had an unshakable impression that his presence was urgently needed back home, so he had returned. His parents said nothing immediately about the revival, but that evening William was one of the first to step forward in response to the gospel invitation.

An early distinctive feature of the Welsh Revival was the repeated outbreaks of *moliannu*, a form of highly energetic praise that united the speaker and the audience. For example, the speaker might say something in praise of the Lord. This was then responded to with an Amen and an expression of praise in sung form by someone in the congregation, leading immediately to an exuberant form of singing and dance. The believers gave loud and free expression to their emotions, while the unsaved people present were correspondingly overcome by feelings of spiritual agony and needed God-given relief.

After taking hold first in Cardiganshire, the revival spread to the county of Montgomery, and later to every part of Wales. It was just as powerful in the South as in the North.

Much of the Welsh Revival was communicated in Welsh. The only major exception to that was in Cardiff, where English-speaking evangelists could be welcomed. The visiting speakers included William and Catherine Booth, who came up from leading missions in Cornwall and led 500 to Christ during their visit. Another 500 were won to Christ in connection with the visit of the evangelist Richard Weaver.

The fact that Wales had so many mining communities meant that some prayer meetings were held far below ground. One subterranean prayer meeting lasted from 6:00am until 2:00pm. Some prayer meetings were hosted by miners on the hillsides, one of them drawing in about 3,000 local people.

In same cases, as happened around Merioneth, nearly all members of the local community became recognised members of a church community. I have had the privilege to witness with my own eyes such a level of community revival overseas. There are many countries in the world where it is not helpful for those concerned to describe where such things happened, and this was one of those. In such a revival, the entire community may gather together in an open-air meeting at the same time, leaving out only those who are too unwell to attend.

The numbers of new converts were recorded carefully by some of the denominations. In the revival, the Calvinistic Methodists recorded 36,190 new converts. The Congregationalists claimed about 36,000 and the Baptists about 14,000. The Wesleyan Methodists gained 4,549 members in 1859-60. The Church of England in Wales gained an estimated 20,000 new communicants. A cautious estimate is, therefore, that the number of new converts in the Welsh Revival was at least 100,000.[5]

While there were fewer prostrations in Wales than in Ulster, there were the same levels of intense conviction and agony of mind. One of the signs of a real revival is that new converts go on with God strongly long after the revival has died down. In this case, it was estimated later that not 1 in 20 people had lapsed from the faith.[5]

Revival in Scotland

The revival in Scotland owed much to what had been happening in America and Ulster. However, it was not as pervasive as it had been in Ulster. This helps explain why the whole revival has been called the Ulster Revival, where what happened in specific places in Scotland and England could then be seen as more like aftershocks.

The Protestant population of Scotland was three times the size of that in Wales, so it was easier there to begin local inter-denominational prayer meetings and to set up large open-air meetings.

The general pattern of the revival was the beginning of regular prayer meetings for revival, typically held on one evening per week. That might increase later to one being held every evening. After much prayer, a large open-air meeting might be organised, perhaps involving a visiting speaker. The widespread sense of being in a revival helped to create a great movement for the wider evangelisation of Scotland.

The first signs of revival were seen in Aberdeen, in the autumn of 1858, where up to a hundred people a night at prayer meetings professed faith in Christ.

The main thrust of the revival came via Glasgow. The influence of the Ulster Revival was felt strongly there, probably due most of all to Glaswegians with business interests in Ulster. Revival became a part of everyday conversation in 1859, and an open-air meeting on 19th August attracted 20,000 people. Many conversions were reported. On 6 September, a crowd of 20,000 gathered on Glasgow Green, where a local butcher called Robert Cunningham was an outstanding speaker.

From Glasgow, the revival fanned out in different directions to the rest of Scotland. People in the more remote parts of the Highlands and some of the Islands may have been slower to hear about the revival but were no less affected by it when it reached them. The Isle of Lewis in the Outer Hebrides, for example, was swept by the revival.

Few places in Scotland were left unaffected. Religious correspondents of London papers were reliably informed at one point that there was no town or village left untouched by the revival between Inverness and Aberdeen.[6] Remote fishing communities were included. There were conversions too at the sites of previous revivals, such as Cambuslang.

The first sign of the revival in Edinburgh was when a notoriously evil factory worker went white-faced and was then overcome at his bench by a sense of fear. He fell to the floor and screamed out so loudly that all the rest of the factory were disturbed. In response, three prayer meetings a day were started at the factory.

The American preacher of revival Professor Charles Finney made a short visit to Edinburgh in November 1859. The events he spoke at were very well attended, and some people were converted. In the following year, evangelistic meetings attracted such huge crowds that the visiting speakers Weaver and Radcliffe had to walk on strong men's shoulders in order to go and minister to some people.

When the Revival reached the Highlands, it had a very special effect in some places on young people or children, who in some cases organised their own prayer meetings.

Young people walked as far as 20 miles to attend a meeting and some children walked as far as 7 miles to get there.

A senior army officer said it was a terrifying sight to see what happened when a person's eyes were opened to the state of their own heart. A journalist in Hamilton (a town in South Lanarkshire, in the central Lowlands) commented that it was a strange sight to see men on bended knees crying out like children for mercy.

There was, of course, some criticism. Some people objected to the prostrations they saw. A complaint was made that the arrangements of normal society had been disturbed, ordinary business interrupted and necessary sleep lost. In reply, Mr Kelman of Port Glasgow said of the prostrations that, though they might be explained by natural causes, the Spirit of God had used them for good purposes. Dr. Buchanan in Glasgow responded that when critics said that society's arrangements were disturbed this assumed that society's arrangements were just what they ought to be, which he did not agree with.

A second wave of revival reached Glasgow in 1861, following the arrival of a young American called Edward Payson Hammond to conduct revival services in Annan on the Solway Firth. The revival spread through several nearby towns.[6, 7]

Revival in England

The revival in England followed those that had already begun in Ulster, Wales and Scotland, and it lasted for several years. There were generally two distinctive phases: a beginning phase when many prayer meetings for revival were started, often with support from several denominations, and then an evangelistic phase that occurred many months later. Awakenings occurred in every part of the country, but not in every place. It would be incorrect, therefore, to call it a general awakening in England.

There was not nearly the same number of prostrations in England that had been seen in Ulster, except when Ulster evangelists ministered. Some Ulster evangelists saw prostration as an evidence of revival power and they, therefore, encouraged it.

Revival in the South of England

Great interest in the revival was shown in both London and Bristol. Lord Shaftesbury helped to bring in legislation that made it possible to hold religious gatherings in unconsecrated places, thereby making theatres available for large-scale Christian events. Another advantage in the larger cities was the availability of public transport, which could convey people to meetings right across their city.

The Baptist minister Charles Haddon Spurgeon worked tirelessly with his London congregation. The church flourished in that time. In Bristol, there was the prayerful orphanage leader George Müller, whose methodical records show that 260 of the children in his care were converted in one year.

Handley Moule, later Bishop of Durham, was a boy at that time living in Fordington near Bristol. He described the revival as coming 'here and there' in England, which well describes its varied impact. Fordington, where Moule lived, was a large parish with no Free Church chapels in it, which therefore gave the (Anglican) vicar considerable freedom to co-ordinate a response to the move of God that was happening there. Hundreds of people were awakened.

People in the counties south of the Bristol Channel accepted the revival vigorously, perhaps reflecting their cultural and geographical closeness to Wales. In Cornwall, a series of missions in different towns led by William and Catherine Booth (Methodists from near Newcastle, and later to be the founders of the Salvation Army) resulted in over 7,000 conversions. One day during this time, Catherine suddenly announced to her husband that she intended to preach from then on. She too saw an outstanding level of response to her preaching.

A Methodist preacher later gave a telling description of Booth's preaching during the mission in Lelant. The preacher reported that those present heard 'a commanding oratory we have never heard excelled' climaxing in the preacher's voice being drowned out 'in the shouts of the saints, the prayers of the people and the cries of the penitents.'[7]

An important factor in the revival was the matter of how well local ministers already co-operated with each other. In Hampshire, for example, this meant that joint prayer meetings and other fruitful events were held in Winchester and Portsmouth, while comparatively little happened in Southampton.

Then there was the warm involvement – or lack of it – from the local Anglican clergy. This could vary from Bath, where the Rector of Bath gave a warm inter-denominational invitation to Anglican prayer meetings, to Salisbury where a 1,000-strong New Year inter-church prayer meeting was held without any co-operation from the Anglican clergy.

The Isle of Wight, the Scillies and the Channel Islands were all reached by the revival, though not as quickly as on the mainland.[8]

Revival in the Midlands and East Anglia

Some shared features of the Revival in the Midlands and East Anglia were the dynamism of many supporters, the strong identity of some local revivals, the great harvests reaped by visiting preachers, the raising up of evangelistic bands (called Hallelujah Bands), and some moves to build or buy large meeting places that were not church buildings. Railway depots were also used as large indoor meeting places.

The energy and courage of some supporters was considerable, as they were often the mainstay of local support that kept going before conversions started happening. Some of these main supporters had position, influence and wealth to make use of, while others did not.

Some key supporters among the Anglican clergy were Alfred Christopher in Oxford, J.C. Ryle in Ipswich and William Pennefather in Barnet. T. Whitehouse, a Methodist minister in Walsall, assumed leadership of the work in *the Black Country* (the highly industrialised area north of Birmingham). The YMCA was also supportive of the revival. Support of the local Mayor could make a big difference, as his permission could open up some of the largest meeting places in the community.

Deliberate opposition was experienced in at least a few places. After John Venn, the Prebendary of Hereford Cathedral, came back from the Ulster Revival and reported on it most positively, his bishop responded by attacking revival to all his clergy. In the village of Daventry in Northamptonshire, visiting evangelists were greeted on arrival with a shower of stones, eggs and rubbish. When two young women wished to set up a united prayer meeting in their village of Little Eaton in Derbyshire, the local clergyman would not support it.

There was a good ending to each of these stories. John Venn welcomed the evangelist William Carter to his schoolrooms, and conversions took place there. In Daventry, a movement of God never witnessed there before was soon underway. The two young women were kindly allowed the use of the United Methodist Chapel in Little Eaton for their union prayer meetings, where attendance at the prayer meetings doubled and then trebled. An evangelist T.M. Hooke from Nottingham helped lead to Christ a local man in South Normanton, Derbyshire, who had visited him in his lodgings with the intent to kill him.

The universities of Oxford and Cambridge were fertile ground for the revival, though not necessarily among local people. Many Oxford undergraduates became Christians as a result of the influence of the student Hay Aitken who came there fresh from fruitful evangelism in Scotland. Daily prayer meetings were started up in the two universities. Two students, namely Francis James Chavasse at Oxford and Handley Moule at Cambridge (who had already known revival in Fordington), went on to be Anglican bishops in later life.

A new strategy used in evangelism were *Hallelujah Bands.* These were groups of new converts drawn from very different backgrounds. They were ideally suited to reach people like themselves. They advertised what they were no longer: dog fighters, drunkards, gamblers, prize fighters, robbers and even bear wrestlers. Their group performances were notable for their extravagant praise, exciting testimonies and ardent exclamations of "Hallelujah!" uttered like gun shots.[9]

Revival in the North of England

The North of England was near enough to the revivals in Scotland and Ulster that some Northerners went to see one of these revivals in action and then reported back with infectious enthusiasm. It also made easier the travel of evangelists from Scotland and Ulster.

Revival took place in many of the large centres of population in the North, as well as in the rural areas. Many people there were employed in factories, mining and cotton mills. There were notable revivals in places such as: Bolton, Blackburn, Bridlington, Chester, Durham, Gateshead, Halifax, Hartlepool, the Isle of Man (which was accessed from the North), Hexham, Leeds, Liverpool, Manchester, Newcastle, Rochdale, Scarborough, Sunderland and York.

Newcastle was one of the first places in the North to see an outbreak of revival. News of the American Revival had stimulated the start of prayer meetings as early as 1858. In the summer of 1859, the town was visited by the Methodist evangelists Dr. & Mrs Palmer who had witnessed the outbreak of revival in 1857 in Hamilton, Ontario. By October 1859 a general awakening had begun.

William Booth was the pastor of Bethesda New Connexion Chapel in Gateshead, near Newcastle. So many conversions took place in that chapel that it was nicknamed 'The Converting Shop'. It is still there, now called Whitehall Road Methodist Church.

Child conversions came before adult ones in Accrington. In 1860, the convicting and converting power of God came down upon children in a Wesleyan Sunday School. By 1863, there were 1,000 pupils and 160 teachers there.

Much of the evangelistic work was done by locals. For example, the minister J.C. Milburn led over a 1,000 people to Christ, including a well-known former secularist (atheist) called J.H. Gordon. In some places like Liverpool, one evangelist came after another, each reaching more people for Christ.

Some visiting evangelists attracted large numbers easily. The Booths and the Palmers from Canada drew in hundreds where they went, while Charles Finney and Richard Weaver attracted thousands.

A third phase of the revival began to emerge in the latter stages of the revival. For example, the people of Glossop in Derbyshire were dismayed to find that their cotton supplies had ceased from the United States, due to the Federal blockade in the American Civil War. This was causing much suffering for those in the cotton-spinning trade. The leaders and converts of the awakening developed relief work to help those in need, during what was called the Cotton Famine in 1861-1865.

One way of explaining the different reception to the revival in England, compared with the rest of the country, is that English Christians were somewhat less spiritually prepared and less expectant for this dynamic move of God. Even Spurgeon was disappointed that his fellow clergy in London did not make more use of the opportunities available. The starting up of prayer meetings did not generally lead to a revival happening locally soon afterwards, which meant that the intercessors had to keep praying without much community response. In a final stage of the revival, the leaders responsible set up evangelistic meetings at which effective evangelists were the speakers.[10]

Richard Weaver was an ex-miner from Shropshire who quickly became an outstanding preacher. His powerful testimony included stories of his experiences as a prize fighter. He was a fascinating person to listen to, and he had a special ability to get through to some of the worst characters imaginable.[1]

Charles Finney was an American professor and an influential theorist on revival as well as a dynamic preacher. He spoke very plainly and must have stretched the polite tolerance of some people in his audiences. He used a very logical method of speaking, carrying along his hearers with the train of his argument. He first exposed unpalatable truths (e.g. about the worldly, the cowardly and the inconsistent). Then he presented the Gospel with its gracious invitations to the penitent person, which led to the opportunity for them to experience God's pardon and peace.[1, 11]

Some consequences for society and the world

- ☑ The whole country was impacted by this revival, helping to turn the United Kingdom into the Christian country, at least in outward forms, that we typically associate with the Victorian era.
- ☑ It has been estimated that almost three-quarters of a million people were won to Christ in the United Kingdom in this revival, based on estimates of 100,000 in Ulster, 30,000 in Scotland, 100,000 in Wales and 500,000 in England. The impacts on society in Ulster and Wales were especially great. Wales became a nation of chapels, with much local life centring around them.[8]
- ☑ The revival was the opening phase of about 50 years of church expansion in the country as a whole.

Thought for Reflection

Some Christians and ministers who were less prepared and eager for revival saw less of it than those who were looking out for it.

Prayer

Lord, please help us to be awake and ready in the country as a whole for whatever You want to do in our day.

6

Aftermath of the 1859 Revival

But Jesus said, "Let the children come to me. Don't stop them!"

(Matthew 19:14)

In the second half of the nineteenth century, the church in the United Kingdom grew larger. This chapter covers the period from 1861 to the turn of the century. 1861 was the year when the new premises of the Metropolitan Tabernacle were opened. The church became what could now be called the world's first mega-church, under the continuing ministry of Charles Haddon Spurgeon (CHS). It was a great consequence of the 1859 Revival, in which Spurgeon and the congregation had played such an active part.

The development of evangelical annual conferences

William Pennefather has already been mentioned as one of the great evangelical Anglicans of the 1859 Revival. Before that he had brought together a small-scale conference of friends in his parish in Barnet in 1856. This conference, with the aim of promoting the spiritual life, followed him when he moved to Mildmay in that year, and it was then held in

Mildmay Park. Lord Shaftesbury was his co-sponsor. The Mildmay Conference became established for the next three decades as the prime annual conference for evangelical leaders and volunteers, with about 3,000 in attendance.

A strong interest in welfare projects started in Mildmay, but it went far beyond it, and it lives on now. From mid-April during the 2020 lockdown due to the coronavirus pandemic, Mildmay Hospital in London E2 took over being London's primary facility for homeless coronavirus patients not needing intensive care.

The 1859 revival resulted in a longing among some evangelical Christians for a deepening of their spiritual life. After being saved from the penalty of sin, glorious possibilities were opened up of living a more holy life, and becoming more like 'the Holy One' Himself. The Holiness Movement came about from those wanting to live and share their discoveries about this life of holiness, in terms of both heart and behaviour.

Conferences with this focus were held in London (Mayfair, 1873), Chamonix in south-eastern France (1873) and Broadlands in Hampshire (July 1874). Conventions were held in Oxford (August 1874) and Brighton (May 1875). These finally developed into the Keswick Convention, first held in Keswick in the Lake District in the summer of 1875. From the descriptions given, the men and women attending these conventions must have felt they were spending days close to heaven.

For a considerable period from then on, the majority of Keswick's leaders and many of its speakers were either leaders or converts from the revival of 1859. Keswick's 'All one in Christ Jesus' motto was derived directly from the benefits of inter-denominational unity that had been so well grasped in the revival. Some great names associated at that time with Keswick include F.B. Meyer, Handley Moule (Bishop of Durham), Theodore Monod (from France, converted in the United States in 1858) and Andrew Murray (from South Africa). James Hudson Taylor, by then known as the great missionary to China, and D.L. Moody the American evangelist both spoke there once.[1]

The special emphasis given to pursuing a 'higher life' of personal holiness led to considerable criticism and opposition in the early days of the movement, but by the 1890s 'Keswick teaching' was so widely regarded that the Convention was by then a mainstream event in the evangelical world. The Keswick Convention continues to this day, although it could not meet as usual in 2020.[1, 2]

C.H. Spurgeon

'CHS' was converted as a boy. He was such a promising young man that he became a 'boy preacher' at the age of 17, and he was first made a pastor at the age of 19. He was both very studious and highly observant of life around him, so he was a delight to listen to. His eager audiences filled the largest halls in London. His congregation, The Tabernacle Fellowship, moved to the newly-built Metropolitan Tabernacle in Elephant and Castle in London in 1861. The output of his ministry was vast. Quite apart from everything else, he answered an average of 500 letters per week. Over-work was the main cause of damage to his health.

The wording of many of his spoken messages is well preserved, and his main points have generally still not lost their power all this time later. Beyond the revival, his capacity for hard work was severely tested by the need to counter disbelieving teaching that was then damaging the Bible-based beliefs of many in the Free Churches, though his focus was on trying to save the Baptist Union as a Bible-believing denomination. He succeeded, though the Tabernacle left the Baptist Union in 1887. The long-drawn out battle with theological liberalism also had a bad effect on his health, rendering him a fragile man while still in his fifties.[3]

Spurgeon gave a short message at many of the Tabernacle prayer meetings in the revival and beyond. The printed record of many of these remains. They are often single-point parables, drawn from his everyday experiences like witnessing road repairs, steam engines in action, having something caught in one of his eyes, or a driverless beer cart that nearly ran him over.[4]

Spurgeon gave about 3,600 sermons and wrote many books, including saying a considerable amount about revival.[5]

Like Queen Victoria, Spurgeon went occasionally for his health to Menton, on the French side of the Mediterranean coastal border between France and Italy. Ventimiglia was the town over on the Italian side. One day at a large social gathering in Menton, at which Spurgeon was present, the British MP John Edward Jenkins persistently ridiculed believer's baptism. Some of the other guests must have looked sideways at the renowned Baptist pastor, but he said nothing.

Towards the end of the gathering, Spurgeon proposed a journey across the border to Ventimiglia on the following day. They all went, where Spurgeon led the group into the cathedral and to the baptistery in the crypt. He invited his anti-immersionist friend from the day before to interpret into English from the Italian guide. The guide explained, through Jenkins' interpreting, that baptism in the early days had always been done by immersion. The stone chamber echoed with laughter, including that of Edward Jenkins. He was quick to realise the significance of what he had just interpreted and admitted that he had been as well 'sold' as any man could be.[6]

The impetus and momentum created for universal education

We turn next to the huge contribution towards education that was achieved substantially by evangelical Christians. They helped to create the conditions for universal education to be enacted in the last quarter of the nineteenth century. This can be seen to have developed in a series of stages:

1. **Sunday Schools** were first begun by Robert Raikes in Gloucester in 1780. Individual Catholics and Protestants had already done such work before this. His own work was done with Wesley's backing. As Raikes was a prominent newspaper proprietor, the formation of Sunday Schools gained public attention. The Schools taught reading and writing as well as Bible knowledge. Having 'school' on a Sunday meant that a child could receive some education despite working manually all week. As for scale, the movement included far more than a million teachers by its centenary in 1880.

2. **The British and Foreign School Society** (as re-named in 1814) was pioneered by an adventurous Quaker called Joseph Lancaster, starting in 1798. He was too autocratic to be contained in an organised movement as it grew, and he was ejected from it in 1814. The schools, which came to be numbered in their thousands, were 'schools for all' and not just for churchgoers. The Bible was a compulsory text, but no teaching or training from it was allowed. This led to some criticism from various directions, because of it being too identified with Nonconformists (non-Anglicans) or not being Christian enough.

3. **National Schools** were directed by an enterprising Anglican Dr. Andrew Bell from 1814, who in his twenties had gone out to India as a chaplain. There were 30,000 of these Anglican schools in England and Wales by his death in 1831.

4. **Factory Schools** came into being after the Factory Act of 1833. Despite their unpromising start and nature, due to government efforts to dilute his factory reforms, Lord Shaftesbury championed these schools for 50 years (he died in 1885). Under the Act, children aged under 9 were prevented from being in factory employment, so they could be educated all day. Children aged under 13 who were employed by factories received two hours of education daily, in facilities provided by the owners. Shaftesbury also saw to it that the principle of daily education of factory children was kept repeatedly before the nation.

5. **The Ragged School Union** was founded in 1844. The concept of the *ragged* child was that this was a child in

too ragged a state to attend Sunday schools. There were plenty of these children in larger cities, many of them being in such a neglected state because of their uncertain parentage. The Union followed the pioneering work done by individuals and organisations in different parts of the country, such as by the minister Rowland Hill and the London City Mission. Shaftesbury became the Union's President from its start. The Ragged Schools were the forerunners of state schools in what would now be called deprived areas.

Thanks to the Christian vision of their founders and champions like Lord Shaftesbury, these schools were far more than just ordinary schools struggling in a difficult district. They were made the base of much else besides, such as: boys institutes, youth clubs, mothers' meetings, coffee rooms, garden clubs, craftsmanship classes, training for future sailors, soup kitchens, facilities for distributing food and clothing to destitute people, as well as giving cooking, sewing and knitting instruction.

6. **The Education Acts of 1870, 1876 and 1880** established universal and compulsory education for children of what would now be called primary age. The legislation was built on a situation where about a seventh of the country's children were already being educated in so-called voluntary schools, as described above.[7]

Tom Barnardo

The Irishman Tom Barnardo was one of the most outstanding Christian child-helpers of the century. The environment of his life's work was to be found in the dark corners of Victorian London, graphically portrayed in Charles Dickens' novels except possibly even worse than Dickens had discovered for himself.

Barnardo was born in Ireland. He was a fun-loving, strong-willed boy who developed a liking for the Enlightenment thinking of Voltaire and Rousseau. However, when the revival reached Dublin in 1859, two of his older brothers became Christians. In the wake of that, he had what he called his 'rebirth' in May 1862.

Dr Henry (Harry) Grattan Guinness was a well-known evangelist and a grandson of Arthur Guinness, the founder of the Guinness brewery business. Grattan Guinness organised that Barnardo and the three other young men in their Young Men's Class could meet in his Dublin home the renowned China missionary leader James Hudson Taylor. All four young men volunteered to join China Inland Mission, though only three of them ever got to China.

Within ten weeks of that meeting, Barnardo began lengthy training in London. He had no thought of studying medicine at that time. As the months went by, Hudson Taylor discerned that Barnardo also had the necessary skills to become a medical missionary. So it was, in 1866 and at the age of 21, Barnardo began a course of medical study at The London Hospital. He was a little older than the other medical students and did not fit in well with them.

From the outset of his time in London, though, Barnardo had been winning respect elsewhere – in the East End. It seemed entirely logical to him that he should volunteer for welfare work, so he became a volunteer of Ernest Street

Ragged School. He had such a way with rough boys that he was soon invited to become the school's Superintendent. However, his own ideas about how to run the school were not altogether well received by his colleagues, and this made him want to try out his ideas where he would be free to lead.

He also became a bold street preacher, using the powers of reasoning that he believed should accompany faith and imagination. Despite the banter he received from his very rowdy audiences, young people were generally glad to listen to him. The extreme roughness of treatment given to him in a pub's back room (the landlord had warned him to stay out of there), left him badly bruised and with two ribs broken. In the six weeks that he took to recover, he found that even that episode had won him the care and respect of those who had harmed him.

During a cholera epidemic in London in 1866, Barnardo bravely volunteered to help. As a volunteer, he saw first-hand the problems not just of cholera but of poverty in the East End. Of the thousands of cholera victims in London, more than 65% of the fatalities happened in the East End. He was not able to forget the visual images of those days, of dead bodies piled up, homes that had lost their breadwinner, and little children left parentless and penniless from a preventable disease.

He started up his own Ragged School and it was to that to which a homeless boy came, called Jim Jarvis. Jim insisted there were 'eaps of other boys, like himself, sleeping rough. Barnardo gave Jim shelter and felt amazed that there could possibly be many other boys like Jim in London, who nobody knew about. He persuaded Jim to take him at night to where other homeless boys could be found. The last part of the journey involved scaling a ten-foot wall. On the sloping roof beyond that, and with no covering, was a *lay* (a place to lay up) where eleven boys were sleeping, aged between about nine and eighteen. This experience was a call to action, just like the pauper's funeral in Harrow had been to young Lord Ashley, later Lord Shaftesbury.

But what about China? Should not the missioner be ready to work wherever his services were fruitful? Jim took Barnardo later to other lays, and sure enough, there were more 'eaps of homeless boys he had told him about. Barnardo was staggered by what he saw, though at that point there was not much he could do for them. He arranged for Jim to be placed in lodgings with a Christian family. Jim later on expressed the wish to emigrate to Canada. Within 15 years, Jim was the prosperous proprietor of a good farm and a respected man in his community.

Not long after that, Barnardo attended a missionary evening, where he was on the front row of the platform because of being a missionary candidate himself. The speaker did not arrive, and Barnardo was persuaded by the organiser to share about his work among those in need in East London. He had never spoken to such a large gathering. He tried to bring it all to a halt, but his fascinated audience kept him talking for an hour. Although he only heard about it later, what he shared that night was reported in the newspapers, and that excited much heated disagreement and discussion among those who heard about it.

That was how Lord Shaftesbury heard about young Barnardo. Shaftesbury had already been President of the Ragged School Union for 23 years by this stage, so he heard about Barnardo who was one of the superintendents. Could it really be that such a great number of street children were slipping through their net? In true Shaftesbury-like style, he decided he must find out the facts. He invited Barnardo to dinner, to which he also invited some of his friends who were interested in social matters.

Conversation at the meal soon turned into a long barrage of searching questions directed at the young man. Where was he born? When did he come to London? What led him to train as a missionary to China? Were the newspaper reports of his speech exaggerated? Could it even be that those youngsters had organised a clever hoax? Was he willing to take them and show them the sights that he had described? Barnardo said he would be glad to do so, whenever they wanted. Lord Shaftesbury replied, “Why not tonight?”

So it was that, near midnight, the party of 15-20 guests took carriages in order to go and find the kind of boys Barnardo had been talking about. At first he did not find any boys. However, he finally found one who then led them to a total of 72 others. The boys all received a meal that night of as much as they could eat, plus a penny each.

Lord Shaftesbury took Barnardo aside and apologised for having doubted him. He encouraged him to pray seriously over the events of that night and to consider whether God was calling him, not to China with all its needs but to work among the homeless children of London. His support for Barnardo’s work after that was assured.

The method of attracting whole groups of boys was simple. Barnardo’s band of assistants went out into the local streets advertising an invitation to poor boys to come to a Sunday event at which they would be fed. Many boys came and clearly enjoyed themselves enough to speak well of what was being done for them.

It was not long before the new work nearly came to a sudden end. The landlord who was renting out to them the large upstairs room for the work suddenly barred them from further entrance. The great success of what was happening upstairs was making the landlord lose custom in his pub downstairs. Barnardo and his group refused to be deterred by this setback. They split up the hospitality and hosted boys in four different venues until another large, rentable space could be found.

Barnardo was a natural leader to whom his co-workers deferred, so there was practically no-one there in the early stages to question the suitability of his methods. He was a young man of great faith, warmth of personality and generosity. He accepted the amounts of money, large and small, that were given to him. However, while being very honest about it, there was no careful book-keeping done in those early stages.

There came a day when a printed article called into question Barnardo's honesty. Without having well-prepared financial records, it was far from easy to dismiss the claims made against him. A thorough-going enquiry found that Barnardo had not been at all dishonest with the money given to him. Instead, the vindication of his good character took the work onto a new level of public regard and scale.

A turning point occurred in the work after a boy called Carrots was refused entrance, due to a lack of anywhere to put him at the Home that he had called at. The boy was found dead soon afterwards. Barnardo and his group were so distressed by Carrots' death that they determined they would never refuse a child entry again. The adoption of their open doors policy, though, brought an in-rush of yet more homeless children. That required the purchase of yet more land, the extension of existing buildings, the development of new ones, and more mouths to feed.

Barnardo's wife Syrie was a great supporter of his work and took a deep interest in it. When aged 18, she had had a life-changing experience under the ministry of Lord Radstock and Dr F.B. Meyer. After that, she threw herself into Ragged Schools work before she ever met Tom Barnardo. Once they had come across each other, their courtship was slow and intermittent, not least because Barnardo was too busy to think about love. Sadly, the public and private face of some great people's lives do not match up. In Barnardo's case, his wife Syrie commended him as a very romantically loving husband.

His marriage to Syrie made it possible to begin the practical care of destitute girls as well as boys. Hard lessons were learned in the first girls' home that they began together. God gave Barnardo a dream one night of housing girls in family cottages within a special village, each with their own 'loving mother'. It was to be an outworking of Psalm 68:6 (AV) 'God setteth the solitary in families.' Following this dream, a Girls Village Home was started, which had nearly 70 cottages in it by the time of Barnardo's death.

The work expanded enormously as the years went by. Barnardo's legacy could be measured by the number of buildings and places where children were looked after by the charity, but the scale of his achievements was far greater than that. He had helped to change the whole approach to child care in the country, and he had done it with faith, energy and fun. It was estimated at his death that 60,000 children had benefited because of all that had been done for unwanted and destitute children. The nation mourned for him in a way only paralleled in those recent years by the death of Queen Victoria four years earlier, in 1901.[7]

Work among children in care has changed out of all recognition since then, and the scale of giving had to grow with that expansion. Barnardo's still functions as a children's charity, though sadly without the outward demonstration of the Christian faith that helped to establish it.

The missions of D.L. Moody and Ira Sankey

The American evangelist D.L. Moody came came from Chicago with Ira Sankey in 1873-75. Their first visit was nearly abandoned soon after their arrival, but for the backing and support of the Baptist minister F.B. Meyer, who had come to Christ as a boy in the wake of the revival of 1859. Sankey played at the piano and led the singing and then Moody preached. They made a powerful and attractive combination to British audiences.

The two men returned to the UK in 1881-83. A significant part of this second visit in England was a mission they led to Cambridge University. Moody had carefully avoided preaching to university students before that, as he felt his lack of education made him ill-suited for the role. On the first evening, the Corn Exchange in Cambridge was packed with sceptical students, who gave him a very hard time. However, a few students were won over, and many came to

Christ by the end of the week. A group of seven of them, called the Cambridge Seven, committed themselves to going out to China with the China Inland Mission, which they did in 1885. This group included the well-known England cricketer C.T. Studd, later the founder of the Africa Inland Mission. Their commitment to Christ in doing such a sacrificial thing was little less than a national sensation.[8]

Moody and Sankey also had a very fruitful time in Scotland on their second visit to the United Kingdom. The different denominations united in working with them, and thousands of people came to Christ.[9]

A new denomination: The Salvation Army

The Salvation Army was founded in 1858, following the renaming of the Christian Revival Society. It was specifically targeted at the down and out. As it worked among people who had been so ravaged by the side effects of alcohol, the Salvation Army took a completely uncompromising attitude to alcohol consumption. The use of a uniform and ranks enabled its officers to convey that there is a spiritual war on and for them to go responsibly and visibly into the darkest places of social deprivation. Its 'war cry' is 'Blood and Fire'. This refers to the blood of Jesus which washes people clean and the fire of the Holy Spirit that purifies Christ's followers and enables them to live lives that are pleasing to God.[10]

The denomination continues to this day, as an international organisation. In the intervening years it has been embraced by the UK as a frontline part of British care for the vulnerable and the 'underdog'. A member of the Royal Family, Princess Eugenie, worked as a Salvation Army volunteer in the coronavirus pandemic. This would have been an unthinkable idea in the past.

The Booths were a fine example of people on fire for God all their Christian lives. They might have remained as Methodists after experiencing such fruitfulness in the revival. However, despite the thousands of people they had helped win to Christ in Methodist churches in that time, it became very clear that the Methodist denominations, most especially their own, did not wish to contain them any longer. Instead, the Salvation Army developed as a separate denomination.

Booth's last speech in 1912 to the Salvation Army ended with these words, which shows well how he viewed his ministry:

> *While women weep, as they do now, I'll fight. While little children go hungry, as they do now, I'll fight. While men go to prison, in and out, in and out, as they do now, I'll fight. While there is a drunkard left, while there is a poor lost girl upon the streets, while there remains one dark soul without the light of God, I'll fight – I'll fight to the very end!*[11]

Missionary work extended

Various new Christian organisations and missions were founded in the years following the revival. The most famous and influential of these missions was probably the China Inland Mission (CIM) founded in June 1865 by Hudson Taylor. While the outstanding quality of his leadership must be acknowledged, it is most unlikely there would have been enough courageous volunteers to leave all and go out to China without the invigorating influences of the revival. Meanwhile, other missionaries continued their own work elsewhere, such as David Livingstone and Mary Slessor in Africa.

Origins of the Labour Party

Christianity played a major part in the origins of a political party representing the working classes. This was at a time when the two competing main parties were both well able to represent the ruling upper class, but were not nearly so understanding or representative of poor people, who are especially precious in God's sight (as indicated for instance by Galatians 2:10).

The first Labour MPs were in fact elected on a Liberal-Labour (Lib-Lab) ticket. This designation meant that they were candidates adopted by a local Liberal association while being financially maintained by their trade unions. The first two Lib-Lab MPs to be elected to Westminster in 1874 both came from a Christian background. Thomas Burt came from a family of Primitive Methodists and was MP for Morpeth for 44 years. Alexander Macdonald, from a Scottish Puritan background, became MP for Stafford.

The first Labour MP to be elected outside of any Lib-Lab arrangement was the Scotsman Keir Hardie, who became MP for West Ham in 1892. Hardie had become a Christian as an adult. He was particularly inspired by the Covenanters, referred to in chapter 1. As regards Liberal-Labour co-operation, he had sadly come to the conclusion that, in times of pressure or difficulty, the Liberals sided with the upper classes and the business managers.

From the outset of his first speech in parliament in 1889, Hardie was most clearly one who cared for the poor, and he became a champion for the unemployed. Although in a minority party of one, he learned quickly that the most effective way to influence the Commons and the Government was by asking searching questions. He attempted to raise the wages of government employees. He urged local authorities to do more for those out of work. He was probably the first MP ever to ask questions in Parliament about the pay and conditions of Westminster staff such as messengers, waiters and doormen.[12]

Some consequences for society and the world

- ☑ The country became identified strongly as being a Christian nation. The Bible played such a prominent part in it that it could be said that the nation was a people of one book.
- ☑ Christians were inspired to take their faith into the public and political sphere. Most of the great welfare movements of the century came from the leadership of evangelicals. Much was achieved for the benefit of children.
- ☑ The Methodists raised up many working class lay preachers in the century, and some of them helped to give the working class their own champions and public voice.

- ☑ The down and out people of the country now had in the Salvation Army a denomination that championed them and cared for them, which continues its work to this day.
- ☑ Keir Hardie, the first Christian MP to thoroughly champion the poor, took his seat in Parliament in 1889.

Thought for Reflection

Christians in these decades repeatedly led the way in welfare matters, both politically and practically. What welfare matters in the United Kingdom most cry out nowadays for Christian-led reforms?

Prayer

Lord, please help us to change society for the better as much as the Christians of the second half of the nineteenth century were bold enough to do.

7

The Welsh Revival of 1904-1905 and beyond

But God showed his great love for us by sending Christ to die for us while we were still sinners.

(Romans 5:8)

It is at this point in the narrative that the tempo rises. This was a twentieth century revival. Much of it happened in Welsh, which adds to its unique quality. Photographs are available of many of those involved. In the intervening time between then and now, some Christians have consciously kept alive the flame of this revival.[1]

This was the third 'Welsh revival', because Wales had been highly impacted in the Great Awakening in the eighteenth century and in the revival of 1859.

The roots of the revival were in the Holiness Movement of the late 1800s, seen both in the United Kingdom and America. There was a quest for more power from God, more holiness and more evangelistic success. The Welsh Revival was infused with feeling and congregational singing, giving ordinary people a large part in it. It was also highly infectious: some people in distant places simply read about it, prayed earnestly and then saw revival break out around them. Some people were converted just from reading a press article about it.

Visiting preachers and ministers from places outside Wales were deeply affected. The atmosphere of revival could sometimes be sensed in the air, even from the moment of stepping off a train. F.B. Meyer and another minister got off a train in Wales and asked a policeman where they could find the revival. "Here, sir!" he replied, pointing to his chest.

Prelude to the revival

In 1891, a prominent barrister and Methodist minister Richard Reader Harris had founded an inter-denominational Pentecostal League of Prayer. In a sermon in Carmarthen in January 1904, he foretold that the church (more widely) was going to see another Pentecost.

In the first few years of the new century, some Welsh ministers prayed earnestly for revival. Christianity in Wales was, in their view, becoming morc institutional and less spiritual. The minister Dean Howell wrote an article, published in December 1902 just weeks before his death, in which he said:

> *What is Wales' greatest need?... Take note, if this was to be my last message to my fellow countrymen... The greatest need of my dear nation and country at this time is spiritual revival through a specific outpouring of the Holy Spirit.*[2]

Seth Joshua, a Calvinist Methodist minister, prayed that God would raise up a young man from the mines or the land to help revive His work in Wales. Little did he imagine that the man of God's choosing would soon have his call confirmed in one of his own meetings.

Outbreak of the revival

The revival's outbreak can be dated to February 1904, in a Calvinistic Methodist chapel in New Quay, Cardiganshire, where Joseph Jenkins was the minister. Being deeply concerned about the spiritual apathy among his young people, he had called a testimony meeting. He was not getting the kind of responses he was hoping to hear until a fresh convert called Florrie Evans stood up and said with a tremor in her voice, "I love Jesus Christ, with all my heart." The youth group were deeply impressed by her sincerity, and an outbreak of extraordinary power then occurred. They became revived from that moment and were soon in demand, with their minister, to talk at testimony meetings throughout the area.

Little more than six months later, Seth Joshua conducted a week of meetings at that chapel in New Quay. He was delighted by the remarkable 'revival spirit' he found there. The assembled people kept re-starting the meeting when he tried to close it, so each of the meetings ended between midnight and 1:00am. He estimated that 40 conversions took place that week.

Seth Joshua spoke of this at the Grammar School in Newcastle Emlyn, and a number of the students were stirred. One of the mature students was Sydney Evans, who told his roommate Evan Roberts about it afterwards. Evan Roberts had been praying for an outpouring of God for 11 years. They determined to accompany Seth Joshua to his next series of meetings, which were at Blaenannerch Chapel, just a few miles north.

At the close of the 7am meeting at Blaenannerch on the Thursday morning, Seth Evans closed with the prayer "Bend us, Oh Lord". The second meeting that morning was an open meeting at which anyone could pray. Roberts was moved from the first meeting to go and kneel at the front. After some others had prayed, he cried aloud, "Bend me, Oh Lord". He said later that he felt overwhelmed by the verse 'God commendeth His love toward us' (Romans 5:8), and a wave of peace and power flooded over him. It made him think about others in Wales and their need of the Saviour.[1, 3]

That day was a turning point day for Roberts. Some leaders present like Joseph Jenkins were somewhat concerned by his intensity. When Roberts went back with the others to Newcastle Emlyn, he withdrew his lifesavings of £200. He began to pray for a little evangelistic team, including his roommate Sydney Evans, who would go speaking across Wales, spreading revival as they went.

Roberts said to Evans, "I have a vision of all Wales being lifted up to heaven. We are going to see the mightiest revival Wales has ever known – and the Holy Spirit is coming soon, so we must get ready." He felt impelled to return to his home village of Loughor, and he gained approval from the Principal to go home and talk to the young people of Moriah Chapel.

His own family were uneasy to see him back home in term-time, alternately laughing and weeping, but the ministers of

Moriah and its daughter church welcomed him. He gained permission to speak to an after-meeting of the youth group on the Monday evening.

Though only 17 young people were present, the anticipated move of God began there as far as Roberts was concerned. He was allowed to hold more evening meetings that week. He urged the young people to prepare for the Baptism of the Holy Spirit. The numbers and the level of response escalated daily, and God's presence seemed to fill the air.

On the Wednesday evening, Roberts spoke at Libanus Church in Gorseinon. It was the first time that he made use of his 'four points', which he repeated many times in the months ahead: (1) Confess any known sin to God and put away any wrong done to others; (2) Put away any doubtful habit; (3) Obey the Holy Spirit promptly; (4) Confess Christ openly.

By the Saturday evening, many parents were also in the crowded church, having seen such a change in their sons and daughters that week. Roberts had a dilemma of his own: Should he go back to his course of study as planned?

On the Sunday, Roberts spoke at the after-meeting and took as his subject 'The importance of obedience'. The meeting lasted until midnight. The people were clearly deeply moved by a sense of divine awe. Roberts had his question answered.

On the Monday evening, Moriah was filled to capacity. Roberts arrived an hour late and read out the last chapter of Malachi, including the stirring words:

> *I will open the windows of heaven for you. I will pour out a blessing so great you won't have enough room to take it in! Try it! Put me to the test! (Malachi 3:10)*

The people were amazed by his boldness and confidence, as he insisted that this passage was about to be fulfilled in Loughor. At midnight, the meeting was still overflowing with a sense of God's power, and it continued for another three hours. The meeting on the Tuesday evening was comparatively hard and cold, though it also went on until 3am.

A Christian publication reported on Wednesday 9th November that a cloud no bigger than a man's hand had arisen in Wales (compare 1 Kings 18:44). The author of the article was Jessie Penn-Lewis, a respected speaker, writer and Keswick contributor. She had learned about what had been happening in a letter from Seth Joshua.

In Gorseinon, the tide was already turning: young people going to the early morning prayer meetings started to gather up those not so inclined to go. Also on the 9th November, an English-language newspaper in Cardiff carried a brief report of the revival happening in West Glamorgan. It said that that the chapel had been besieged with people. The young preacher had spoken in Welsh and gave impassioned, unprepared speeches that had the most stirring effect upon his listeners.[4]

An increased impact

On Friday 11th, Moriah Chapel was overcrowded with over 800 people. Many spent a long time on their knees in an agonised spiritual state. A newspaper reporter from Cardiff was amazed by what he saw. Many people were still talking in the road as he walked away after the end of the gathering at 4:25am. His article received wide circulation in Wales and beyond. A local minister reported that the community had turned into a praying multitude. The only theme of popular conversation there was Evan Roberts.

At Tregaron, a fourth Keswick-style convention was held, organised by Jenkins and others. The programme soon gave way to the 'freedom' of an open meeting, and 'much blessing' was reported. By the end of December, Jenkins and his friends had caught up with the unstructured nature of the revival and were enjoying the full effect of it.

The movement was felt strongly in Pembrokeshire before the end of 1904. People were talking about God in trains, shops and banks. 20,000 people were enrolled as church members in those first weeks, and the number of those converted would have been larger than that.

Capable teachers like Seth Joshua and Keri Evans went about giving valuable and stabilising teaching. They made some useful distinctions to their audiences, for example: that *conviction* (a recognition of personal need for forgiveness) was not the same as *conversion* (an act of the will in turning to Christ); and that *awakening* (being roused collectively from a dead or sleepy state to a sense of sin and the need to respond to God) was not the same as *repentance* (a complete change of direction, taken personally, from sin to Christ).

Roberts later spoke at Tabernacle Chapel (Congregational) in Pontycymer, a village north of Bridgend. The movement from there swept through the Rhondda valley, which went on long after he had left it.

In the second week of December, local newspapers reported that revival was spreading rapidly in North Wales, beginning with inter-denominational prayer meetings and leading to the setting up of preaching services and open meetings. The results were the same as in the South: the enlivening of church members, followed by the conversion of outsiders and the virtual elimination of drunkenness and swearing.

Consistent with his self-effacing convictions, Roberts declined invitations to Cardiff, but extraordinary scenes occurred there anyway. At the Baptist Tabernacle, now called Tabernacle Chapel, there were 33 conversions at the New Year's Eve service, which took the total of those recently professing faith at the church to 260.

By the end of 1904, two months after the start of the revival, church membership had increased in South Wales by 34,131. In January, Roberts continued in the Swansea Valley, drawing crowds of 2,500–3,000.

In North Wales, a local minister rejoiced that the police had nothing to do, as the streets were so quiet. Quarrels arising from a recent strike had been settled, and the whole community there was uplifted.

A visit to North Wales by Jenkins and a group of singing girls resulted in an extraordinary stir. A quarry-man turned teacher called Evan Lloyd-Jones received an immediate call to ministry. Lloyd-Jones went on to become almost as famous in North Wales as Evan Roberts was in the South.

Numbers of people were flocking into the churches in North Wales, and meanwhile visitors were coming in from much further away such as William Booth, F.B. Meyer and Campbell Morgan. Campbell Morgan, pastor of Westminster Chapel in London, said that he had never seen anything like it in his life and that it was a movement in which the true forces and functions of the church were being exercised. Lord Pontypridd remarked that the revival advertised and funded itself, without posters, hired halls or salaries.

People came to meetings not knowing whether Roberts would speak even when he was expected to do so. Quite often he would say little, maybe speaking for 10-15 minutes. He might say nothing, or not arrive at all.

A spiritual confrontation occurred when Roberts was with 600 people in a Methodist chapel in Llansamlet. He became aware of two young mockers present, and he called on them to yield to the divine influence, which they refused to do. The response from those present was a hurricane of audible prayer which tore through the building. There appears to have been no more mocking from the two young men after that. Congregations knew plenty by then about the power of simultaneous, focused prayer.

Roberts had a gift for exposing untruth. There was more than one occasion when he publicly exposed deceit that he could not have known about beforehand, and afterwards those he had named admitted that he had been correct.

Girl groups accompanying a travelling speaker sang solos, duets and spoke directly to female *penitents* (those seeking God after the meetings, who were conscious of past sin). There was repeatedly a sense of divine awe in the congregational singing. Singing might be led by *anointed* individuals (those with the power of the Holy Spirit clearly upon them), such as Annie Davies.[5] The vital role of women generally in this revival should not be underestimated.

Congregations also learned to sing in the Spirit, creating a remarkably coherent sound. They also loved singing hymns. One of their favourites was 'Here is love vast as the ocean', sung of course in Welsh.[6] It has been called the love song, and the signature tune, of the Welsh Revival.

There was also a notable oneness of spirit. Prominence was given to prayer, and a passionate love for the Bible was evident. The level of spontaneity was difficult for ministers to manage, as it was so different from their usually more organised services.

The revival reached its highest point in early 1905. The numbers of converts were listed regularly in the papers. Total numbers of converts in the revival rose to 100,000 in six months. 80,000 of those people were still in church membership in 1914, despite loss of numbers to mission halls and emigration to America. The expression *mission hall* conveys well the belief that the church is the gathered people rather than the building they meet in.

Public criticisms levelled at Roberts began, which he did not reply to. The adverse effect these were having on him was not immediately apparent. By early 1906, he was so exhausted that he stepped back from everything. The group of capable ministers, teachers and evangelists who had not been the subject of the reporters' attention carried on without him. A steady phase followed, in which a more permanent work was done, involving the building up of new converts and further outreach.

Fewer cases went through the courts. At New Year 1905, the Swansea Court did not have one case of drunkenness to deal with, an all-time record. Magistrates in several towns were presented at court with white gloves, signifying that there were no cases to try on that day. Convictions for drunkenness in Glamorgan in 1906 were just over half the number recorded in 1903.

Stocks of Bibles were sold out. Prayer meetings were held in mines, trains, trams and offices. Business managers reported a change in the conduct of their employees. Some working people brought back to their home their elderly parents from the *workhouse* (a very basic place of shelter for the poor). Longstanding debts were paid, stolen goods were returned, and fighters and gamblers were converted. Ploughboys stood up in church meetings and spoke in clean and standard Welsh.

Students at University College of North Wales in Bangor, Gwynedd in northwest Wales, were touched enough that lectures were abandoned one day, and 300 gathered for afternoon prayer. In the evening, they marched to the crowded Tabernacle in the city.

There were many times when children took part in public meetings, prayer, singing and exhortation. In some places, children organised their own prayer meetings in barns, woods and even empty pigsties.[4]

There was an unusual pit strike, in which the pit ponies would no longer respond to the miners, who were not shouting and swearing as they had done in the past.[7]

Combined church membership of the biggest Nonconformist denominations increased by 80,000. Anglican churches gained fewer people during the revival but more afterwards. The Quakers saw their largest church building in Wales, seating 2,000, packed out on some occasions. Comments from High Church sources and the Roman Catholic Church were generally positive.

The Welsh politician David Lloyd George, who was MP for Caernarvon Boroughs and subsequently Prime Minister from 1916 to 1922, compared the revival in Wales to an earthquake and a tornado.[5]

Evan Roberts

The story of the life of Evan Roberts is both an inspiration and a caution for those who watch and pray for revival. A childhood friend David Grenfell, who later became a well-known politician, later described him from those days as wise, easy-going, kind, idealistic and moral. He saved the life of his brother Dan twice. He also saved a friend Jenkin Evans from serious trouble in a stream even though he (Evan) was unable to swim at the time.

He had to leave school after his father broke his leg in a colliery (mining) accident and needed assistance. He worked in the mines from the age of 12 to 19. His Sunday School responsibilities developed into him becoming the Superintendent. He had aspirations to become a minister from the age of 15, but he was put off by seeing how young candidates lost their spirit when in ministerial training.

There was the very sobering experience of a pit explosion in January 1897, which killed several of his workmates and scorched his Bible which he had kept stored underground. He was left unharmed because he was on a different shift. He liked to use his Bible later as a visual aid.

His popularity at the colliery with his workmates led to him becoming a union man representing his workmates to the management. He also became a member of the mine's rescue team. He was seen as an outstanding Christian among his family, friends, workmates and fellow churchgoers.

After losing his job at a coal mine in 1902 because of a strike, he became an apprentice blacksmith to his uncle. He lived next door to the forge. He concluded, however, that his apprenticeship was a hindrance to God's calling on his life, and in December 1903 he offered himself for the ministry. The need for more education and training was why he was a student in the Grammar School in Newcastle Emlyn, in preparation for ministerial training at Trefecca College.

He had been impressed by an exhortation he had received well beforehand to be ready whenever God comes, so he was a man waiting to respond when Seth Jones came to Newcastle Emlyn. He had also had a series of experiences in the springtime before that when, over a three-month period, God had woken him up night after night. He was taken up into fellowship with God for hours at a time.[8]

Once alerted by the visit of Seth Jones, his prompt action of going back to his own young people in Loughor, to take the revival to them, launched him into being the main figurehead of the revival in South Wales especially. He was still a young and untrained man.

There seems to be an absence of reference to anyone supervising him, or even that he regularly sought advice from the experienced ministers working with him. He and his companions seemed unaware until afterwards of the huge spiritual battle they had stepped into.

Roberts hated anything that promoted him personally, as he wanted people to focus on Jesus Christ. He kept away from reporters when he could. As the revival continued, he became more conscious of spiritual obstacles during meetings, which led to some unhappy incidents (e.g. him saying that it was pointless praying for a particular person).

In less than two years, he had become the world's most publicised preacher, but he was burned out from nervous exhaustion. He had missed meals, had many long days (some of them 20 hours long), unwelcome amounts of attention, and (worst of all) some strong criticism from a few who could have been supporting him.

Criticism began first when observers began to note instances of his unusual conduct in meetings. His critics suggested there were other things wrong with him too. His gift of discernment left him open to charges of clairvoyance. Rumours of sexual misbehaviour or of financial irregularity failed to stick.

The hardest criticisms of all came from Peter Price, the evangelical minister of Bethania, a Congregational chapel in Dowlais near Merthyr Tydfil. Price wrote a stinging letter that was published in the Cardiff papers in January 1905. He claimed that there had been two revivals, a true and a sham one, where the chief figure of the sham one was Roberts.

He asked if the lay preacher was the fourth member of the Godhead, given the way he spoke. He said there were other miners with more intellectual capacity and spiritual power. He urged Roberts 'and his girl-companions' to withdraw.

The public responded overwhelmingly in support of Roberts, who himself did not reply to these criticisms. He was hurt, though. In early February, he followed medical advice to have some rest. Reports of his ill-health soon began to circulate.

By early 1906, he was suffering from nervous exhaustion and had to stop. His life's work was over, even though those close to him still held him in awe. Some of his co-workers like Sydney Evans also experienced nervous exhaustion. In April 1906, Roberts retired to convalesce in the Penn-Lewis home in Leicester, where he was supported financially by friends. It took him a long time to recover his health. He then largely led the life of a recluse, giving himself to prayer and writing poetry, and refusing all media interviews. He took part in a series of prayer meetings in Gorseinon in the mid 1920s. From 1930 until his death in 1951 he lived quietly in Cardiff.

Roberts' vision of 100,000 people coming to Christ in Wales was fulfilled in just a few months, and the revival impacted many other parts of the world.[3, 5]

Awakenings in Ireland

News of the Welsh Revival was warmly welcomed by believers in Ireland, including some with memories of the 1859 Revival. Presbyterian church leaders were at first cautious about the nature of the revival they were hearing about. However, by New Year 1905, all editorial comments were well-disposed.

Days of prayer and the arrangement of prayer meetings multiplied in Ulster and Dublin. The prayer meetings were followed up with some fruitful evangelistic campaigns.

An awakening soon followed among Methodists in Lurgan, which reached the Presbyterians too. People who were not regular churchgoers were attracted, adults and children were converted, communicant lists increased by 50%, churches were packed and the pubs were correspondingly empty.

Local awakenings then spread to Antrim, Armagh, Londonderry, Down, Fermanagh and Tyrone. In Newtownards, a single church listed 1,300 enquirers. In Belfast, there was a flurry of evangelistic activity. The evangelists John McNeil (from Scotland) and Billy Spence each saw hundreds of conversions. Seth Joshua was invited to address the (Presbyterian) Irish General Assembly.

The awakening in Ulster spread to other denominations, so that the Quakers, Salvation Army, Baptists, Moravians and Congregationalists all reported an upsurge in numbers. In Clough (otherwise spelled Clogh), County Antrim, Presbyterian and Baptist churches ran a joint series of meetings in which hundreds professed conversion.

Tobermore in County Londonderry was the scene of a classic sequence of revival. Fred Gibson accepted being the minister of First Presbyterian Church there and soon concluded that the community was morally and spiritually dead. He made a covenant with God to seek revival, signed it and started preaching in his church accordingly. Despite much early resistance, an intense conviction of sin came down on the local people, and even some *hardened* sinners (people seemingly most unlikely to change their ways) were converted.

A 'glorious revival' occurred in the southern provinces of Ireland, among the small Protestant congregations scattered there. Irish Episcopalians in the South as well as in the North were gratified by the signs of revival in their parishes. In Dublin, there were hundreds of conversions in evangelistic meetings.

The awakening in Ireland was not as dramatic as the one in 1859, but it was lasting. It helped to produce a great number of candidates for ministry and overseas mission. It also helped to prepare Ireland spiritually, as people of faith, to endure suffering (as in Hebrews chapter 11) in the devastating losses of the First World War. The awakening also spread over to the Isle of Man.[6]

Awakenings in Scotland

News of the Welsh Revival spread by the end of 1904. By early 1905 special services were being held all over the land, and in every county there was a charged spiritual atmosphere[7]. The press reported awakenings in various parts of Scotland. Some of the first outbreaks of revival involved the participation of veterans of the 1859 Revival, as in Cockenzie, East Lothian, and in Blairgowrie, in Perth and Kinross.

Scottish Christians were generally eager to respond, and many interdenominational prayer meetings were held. Some Welsh speakers, like J.J. Thomas brought some of the fire of the Welsh Revival to Glasgow. In Motherwell, there were so many seekers that even the surrounding streets were crowded.

The pattern in the crowded gatherings was sometimes to have almost no preaching. Spontaneous testimony meetings resulted in the winning to Christ of many outsiders and lapsed church members.

The awakening spread from Motherwell to Cambuslang, scene of revivals in 1742 and 1859. Hundreds professed conversion in Stirling. Remarkable stirrings were also reported in Falkirk, Inverkeithing and Coatbridge.

In Glasgow, a party of Welshmen were participants in an awakening that was similar in form to that in Wales, in which 500 converts professed faith publicly. The large Tent Hall went on being filled nightly for months, and 5,000 enquirers were instructed. From the city centre, the revival spread to the suburbs and the satellite towns.

A lively prayer movement began in Dumbarton and Clydebank, leading to open-air meetings for outsiders. Methodists reported 2,000 coming to the Lyceum in Govan.

In Leith, the port of Edinburgh, evangelistic meetings were packed nightly for 12 weeks. There was great spontaneity, and the extraordinary quality of the praying resulted in many conversions. I have seen the powerful place of such praying in the Cambridge mission that is described in chapter 8.

Edinburgh shared in the general movement of revival. Joseph Kemp, the pastor of Charlotte Chapel in Shandwick

Place, visited Wales in late 1904. At the chapel's watchnight service on New Year's Eve, great zeal in prayer led to a deep conviction of sin. The local press documented the ongoing story, as marches were organised along Princes Street, and evangelistic rallies were held. More than 1,000 were converted in that movement.

J.J. Thomas visited the Borders, and revival was reported in Hawick and Galashiels. The awakening spread to the North East of Scotland, notably to Dundee and Aberdeen. In Aberdeen, there was a great and fruitful evangelistic crusade led by Gipsy Smith in 1906.

The awakening spread through churches in the Highlands. There were also some notable moves of God in the Orkneys, Shetlands and smaller islands like Tiree. On the Isle of Lewis, a movement that started in 1903 continued until about 1912.

The Americans R.A. Torrey & C.M. Alexander led evangelistic campaigns and huge meetings in various cities such as Edinburgh, Aberdeen, Glasgow and Dundee, in which thousands of people were won to Christ.[8]

Awakenings in England

While the special quality of the Welsh Revival exceeded what happened later in England, it needs to be noted that awakenings in England were under-reported nationally at the time and were subsequently rather lost from historical attention.

Due to the presence of Welsh immigrants, word-of-mouth news came quickly to cities like Liverpool and Manchester.

Prayer meetings in Lancashire multiplied. Evidence of revival soon followed. In Wigan, the Holy Spirit came down on crowds as large as 5,000 at a time. A Methodist circuit in and around Bootle reported an increase of 700 in their membership. In Liverpool, the Welsh practice was followed where everyone prayed aloud together. There were awakenings in Birkenhead and Blackpool. Gipsy Smith held a series of evangelistic meetings in Manchester, concluding with a great midnight meeting for drinkers and drunkards.

Evan Roberts went very little to England, but he addressed Welsh-speaking residents in Liverpool. His visit was attended by some problems as well as blessings. In one meeting, he stopped speaking to address whoever it was in the audience who was trying to hypnotise him, which proved later to have been the case. In other meetings there were some interruptions and incidents, as well as some painful silences from him. The press generally responded well to the man and his message.

Over the Pennines in Hull, an awakening there was so great that the Methodists called Hull a 'converting furnace'. There were also great awakenings in Halifax and Sheffield. In Bradford, the great movement of the Spirit there was compared to what had happened in the time of John Wesley.

There were other remarkable awakenings further north. Residents of the colliery town of Hirst, Northumberland, related well to what had happened in Welsh colliery towns. Hundreds were converted, including some being overwhelmed by the Holy Spirit. The awakening then spread rapidly through other mining towns and villages.

As many as 1,000 professed conversion in Newcastle in one week. In South Shields, 400 people professed conversion. Spencer Watson perceptively described Sunderland as 'ripe for blessing', as it soon became a Pentecostal rallying point. John McNeil preached to standing-room-only gatherings in Durham, and the largest halls were overcrowded to hear the evangelist W.E. Geil in Bishop Auckland. In Ellenborough, Cumbria, a third of the town's population were converted. Hundreds were converted in Barrow-in-Furness in just two months.

News of the Welsh Revival caused many in the Midlands to pray. A Birmingham city mission had already been planned for January 1905. By March, Methodist journalists were reporting a great awakening there ('Wales in Birmingham') and throughout the Midlands. Prayer meetings in Nuneaton were followed by a 'glorious revival' involving hundreds of conversions.

An awakening began in Nottingham without the help of church leaders, advertising or missions. Volunteers (i.e. laymen) organised meetings that gave time for praise, prayer, testimonies, fellowship and opportunities for decisions. In nearby Bulwell, there were 386 conversions in 8 weeks.

Awakenings occurred in places such as Bedford, Northampton, Kettering, Rugby, Stratford-upon-Avon, Leicester, Loughborough, Hereford and Monmouth (across in Wales).

Prayer meetings multiplied in Gloucester, and a move of God swept the town. An unpleasant confrontation occurred when an angry crowd spilled out from the pubs upon a procession of thousands of singing people.

There were united prayer meetings in Bristol from early January 1905, and news of 'Revival in Bristol' was soon reaching distant parts of the country. In Kingswood, the scene of revival in the previous century, more than 3,000 professed conversion.

In Colchester, in East Anglia, some churches followed the Welsh example of having some midnight evangelistic rallies. 800-900 attended prayer meetings in Ipswich, and there was a harvest of conversions. Churches in Lowestoft gained many new members, and those in King's Lynn reported the beginning of an awakening.

Cornwall, with its Celtic connections, was deeply stirred by the Welsh Revival. Newquay and Penzance were especially touched. Other places in the South West that were deeply impacted included Falmouth (with 750 professed conversions), Devonport, Plymouth, Exeter, rural Devon, Barnstaple, Swindon, Bath, Wellington and Weymouth.

There was a move of God in an Anglican church in Shirley, Southampton, where T.W.H. Jacob was the Vicar. There were over 500 enquirers during a mission led by Frederick and Arthur Wood, which was followed by further successful missions there. The awakening was also felt in the rest of Hampshire and on the Isle of Wight.

The movement in Sussex reached Hastings in March. Reading, Woking, Watford and Tunbridge Wells were among the places touched by it. In Deptford, a Methodist Circuit more than trebled in size from 190 members in 1903 to 729 in 1905.

In London, united prayer meetings were held from January 1905. F.B. Meyer hosted a conference for ministers and others to discuss revival, in which the singing of praise repeatedly overwhelmed the programmed speakers. The evangelistic phase in London included a Torrey & Alexander campaign, as well as missions organised by the Bishop of London. In Leyton, Gipsy Smith led a campaign in which 800 were converted. Meetings in Ilford produced hundreds of enquirers. A great wave of blessing was also felt in the west of London.[9]

Some consequences of the revival

☑ The Welsh Revival caused preaching to become more challenging, and churches were revitalised. It particularly reached young people. Women became much more prominent in Christian meetings and in ministry to individuals. They often led meetings. The closeness of Christian fellowship that people experienced in that time helped to add to the warmth towards one another that is now part of Welsh identity and community life.

☑ About 100,000 came to faith in Jesus in Wales. It inspired passionate prayer, and it spread widely elsewhere. Impacts of revival were felt in the rest of the United Kingdom and in many other parts of the world including: the United States, Africa (notably Algeria and South Africa), Australia, Austria, the Balkans (especially Bulgaria), China, France, Germany, Hungary, India, Italy, Japan Korea, New Zealand, Nordic countries (especially Norway and Sweden), Poland, Russia and Slovakia.[10]

Thought for reflection

Evan Roberts' much-repeated four points were: (1) Confess any known sin to God and put away any wrong done to others; (2) Put away any doubtful habit; (3) Obey the Holy Spirit promptly; (4) Confess Christ openly.

Prayer

Lord, please help me to follow these points carefully myself.

8

The rest of the twentieth century

For I will pour water upon him that is thirsty, and floods upon the dry ground.

(Isaiah 44:3, KJV)

It has been seen that the twentieth century began with a mighty revival in Wales, which then spread to other parts of the country. All this was a good preparation for the devastation of war that would soon break upon the world.

There were no further national revivals in the UK in the twentieth century, though there were some local revivals. Other moves of God occurred, some of which are mentioned because of their continuing significance.

This was arguably the most secular century in world history. In two world wars, three of the most mission-minded nations (the United Kingdom, Germany and latterly the United States) were pitched into brutal warfare, costing millions of lives and damaging much more besides, including the fervour of many professing Christians. Many men who returned alive from World War I came home having lost their spiritual life in the trenches. Bold hopes and plans about completing the work of world evangelisation, as discussed at the Edinburgh Missionary Conference of

1910[1], were severely set back. The rise of secularising forces such as Fascism and Communism led to strong persecution of Christians in some countries. Increased confidence in atheism arose among some western intellectuals, such as Jean-Paul Sartre in France and Bertrand Russell in the United Kingdom.

The Azusa Street Revival in the United States and the beginnings of the Pentecostal Movement

The Azusa Street Revival of 1905 began in Los Angeles in the United States at almost the same time as the Welsh Revival of 1904-1905. Some of the leaders of the two revivals were in communication with each other. Parallels in their leadership policy are evident, such as the long, unstructured meetings that allowed the Holy Spirit as much freedom to move as possible. The great revival in the United States, beginning in that interracial church, led to the foundation of the Pentecostal Movement worldwide.

Outpouring in Sunderland and beginnings of the Pentecostal Movement in the UK

Alexander Boddy was at that time Vicar of All Saints Church in Monkwearmouth near Sunderland. Revivals had taken place there in 1821, 1859 and 1905. As noted already, Spencer Watson described it as ripe for (more) blessing in 1905.

Boddy was born in 1854. He was appointed Vicar of All Saints in 1884 by the J.B. Lightfoot, then Bishop of Durham. Boddy had an enquiring mind, was a seasoned travel author and was open to Christian traditions other than his own. Spiritually, he had the broad shoulders needed for an inclusive style of leadership in the Pentecostal outpouring and for responding to the forms of opposition that followed.

Boddy visited the Welsh Revival in 1904. He loved what he saw, including the freedom in worship. He even shared a pulpit with Evan Roberts at one moment. He came back encouraged by Roberts to 'believe the promises'. He shared the fire in Sunderland churches, which included various preaching engagements and an open-air event that 15,000 people attended. Handley Moule, his bishop, was very supportive, just as he had been of the Welsh Revival.

Thomas Barratt was a Welsh-born Norwegian minister based in Oslo. He had gone over to New York seeking Methodist financial help for a city mission project of his in Oslo. He was not getting very far with this quest and then happened to learn about news of revival in Los Angeles. He received the Baptism of the Holy Spirit there.

Boddy visited Barratt and his church in Oslo in early 1907. He was amazed to be surrounded by young Norwegians speaking in tongues and seeing visions. He himself received the Baptism but did not speak in tongues.

In the same season, Catherine Price in Brixton, London, was the first person in the UK known to have received a Pentecostal experience of the Holy Spirit. This happened in connection with a convention conducted by four Welsh ministers from the Welsh Revival. She spoke in tongues there in three recognisable languages (Mandarin Chinese, Indian and Italian), similar to what happened on the Day of Pentecost. A minister sitting next to her asked her if she knew the language she has just been speaking. She shared the interpretation in English and, she later said, 'the result was conviction, confession, and wholehearted yieldedness to the Lord Jesus all over the hall'. Many healings occurred later in meetings held in her own rooms that summer, where people went to pray and wait on God.[2]

It later became known that other individuals in Wales, the South Coast and the North of England had also received during the summer the Baptism of the Holy Spirit and spoke in tongues.[3]

Thomas Barratt was invited by Boddy to go to Sunderland, and he finally arrived and stayed from 31st August to 18th October 1907. He led nightly meetings from 1st September. In the course of that time, Boddy's wife Mary and teenage daughters received the Spirit and started speaking in tongues. In those early days, there was also some holy laughter and some repetition of first syllables (as of the word 'Glory') which sounded animal-like to some.

An outstanding debt on the church hall was immediately cleared, and there remains until now at All Saints Church a stone inscription which captures that moment in time:

SEPTEMBER 1907
WHEN
THE FIRE OF THE LORD
FELL
IT BURNED UP THE DEBT.[4]

The local press picked up the story at the end of September, and the news of it reached some London papers a few days later. The press coverage was, in Boddy's description, 'grotesque', but it nonetheless sparked widespread and deep interest. Visitors started coming from all over the country. By the end of October, the news was reaching other countries like the United States, India, South Africa and Jamaica.

The news of what was happening must have seemed fascinating to some, who then came to see for themselves. However, the Christian magazines *The Christian* and *The Life of Faith*, and in particular the feature writer Jessie Penn-Lewis were firmly critical of what they heard. Penn-Lewis, who with her husband was *harbouring* (giving a protected home to) Evan Roberts in his convalescence, had concluded that 'other spirits' might be encountered in revival. Boddy's attempts to conciliate her were not successful. She never did go to Sunderland.

Reader Harris did go there. He was the respected barrister and minister who had foretold a Pentecost-like move of God before the outset of the Welsh Revival. He had set up the Pentecostal League of Prayer back in 1891. The League had regular prayer meetings in nearly 150 locations, one of which met in Boddy's vicarage. Harris saw the genuineness of the Baptism of the Holy Spirit as being evidenced by entire sanctification (by which he meant achieving complete holiness and Christlikeness). This idea was close to teaching that had been given widely by John Wesley on *Christian perfection* (where the heart of the believer is cleansed from inbred sin).[5]

Harris did not agree with Barratt's emphasis that the genuineness of the Baptism should be evidenced outwardly, by speaking in tongues. Boddy actually emphasised the evidence of the love of the Spirit more than tongues, but he sided with Barratt in the dispute.

Boddy's notes for November recorded that a 'prominent worker' called Smith Wigglesworth arrived that month from Bradford with a friend. Wigglesworth was the Leader of the Bowland Street Mission in Bradford. He was a man of great faith and was very clear about what he was seeking. He was aware of mixed views among his Salvation Army colleagues in Bradford about this movement, and he was ready to go straight home if he needed to. He had had a life-changing healing some years previously, but he had concluded that he was not living in the full power of Pentecost or had the evidence of 'signs following' (Mark 16:20, KJV).

During his visit lasting some days, Wigglesworth wrote that he found 'the enemy very busy discouraging believers'. He finally received the baptism (of the Holy Spirit) in the vicarage kitchen, ministered by two people laying hands on him. As he put it, 'the fire fell and burned in me till the Holy Spirit revealed absolute purity before God....'[6] Once he was home again, his wife Polly could hardly believe it was her husband speaking the first time she heard him preach after that.[7]

Wigglesworth remained a loyal friend to the Boddys after that and he was a contributor of articles to them over the following decades, as his ministry spread across the English-speaking world. He was a one-off and legendary itinerant minister who touched and helped people of many denominations. He happily described himself as a Pentecostal.

He had a strong dislike of newspapers, which was clearly very important to him in his walk with God and his concentration on reading the Bible. However, it could be very difficult, for those who have tried to copy his example, to promote radical social transformation without keeping a close interest in current affairs. He is especially remembered for some remarkable healings that occurred in the course of his ministry.

Leading on from what they had learned about what God had been doing in Asuza Street and Sunderland, there was an outpouring in the mining town of Kilsyth, among believers meeting regularly in a converted theatre called Westport Hall. God had moved in power in Kilsyth before. The town became the main centre for the new movement in Scotland.[8] The church is now called Kilsyth Church of God. Soon there were many Pentecostal assemblies across the United Kingdom.

God raised up two brothers from the miners in Wales, called Stephen and George Jeffreys. They each went on to see hundreds converted at a time and many healings in their evangelistic campaigns. 1,100 were converted in just one meeting led by George Jeffreys in Bournemouth.[9, 10]

Invitations to Alexander and Mary Boddy, like the one that came from Kilsyth, were coming in from different directions by the turn of 1907/1908. He also wrote many articles. They hosted Sunderland conferences from 1908 to 1914, which became the leading convention in Europe for Pentecostals. The Boddys spoke at other Pentecostal conventions from 1908, besides making many visits elsewhere.

Visitors and participants in the conference included: Frank Bartleman from the Asuza Street Revival, Arthur Booth-Clibborn (son-in-law of William and Catherine Booth, who came regularly as an interpreter and speaker), Cecil Polhill (one of the Cambridge Seven, described in chapter 6, and co-founder with Boddy of the Pentecostal Mission

Union), Stanley Frodsham from Bournemouth (a great chronicler of the Pentecostal Movement), Stephen and George Jeffreys from Wales (who went on to lead the Elim churches in the UK) and Howard Carter (who went on to lead the Assemblies of God in the UK).

Boddy edited an affirmatively oriented paper, called *Confidence*, from 1908 to 1926. It became the main agency of news for British Pentecostals and important to others throughout the English-speaking world. It was needed partly because he was having difficulty getting material published in existing Christian newspapers and magazines, and partly because by that time he was writing so much.[11]

Pentecostalism as a new denomination

Alexander Boddy had wished to see spiritual renewal reaching throughout the denominations. However, that did not happen until at least a generation later, and Pentecostalism was therefore obliged to develop as a separate entity. People first heard about the Sunderland revival through secular press coverage, which was fairly impartial whilst talking up the unfamiliar phenomenon of speaking in tongues. Christian responses alternated mostly between indifference and outright disagreement with the 'Tongues Movement', as some called it.

By the end of 1906 it had become apparent to those in Sunderland that a new move of God had begun there, the main emphasis of which was a personal spiritual experience of receiving 'the Baptism of the Holy Spirit', invariably accompanied by speaking in tongues and other clear evidences. Much was developing abroad meanwhile in other countries, notably in the United States, some Nordic countries (Denmark, Finland, Norway and Sweden) and India.[12]

The Pentecostal Movement has since then become a huge movement worldwide, with over 250 million members. Pentecostal churches are now among the most active of church groups in the UK today. Among the Pentecostal denominations now in the country, the Redeemed Christian Church of God (RCCG) has over 850 parishes.[13] Elim Pentecostal Church (Elim) has nearly 650 churches in the UK and Ireland.[14] The Assemblies of God (AOG) Great Britain has more than 500 churches in over 700 locations in the UK and Ireland.[15]

Revivals in East Anglia and North-East Scotland in 1921

A mission in Lowestoft was planned for March 1921, to be led at London Road Baptist Church by Douglas Brown, a Baptist Minister from Balham in south London.

Although Brown had promised months previously to lead the mission, it is apparent from his words at the Keswick Convention afterwards that he had some unspoken reluctance about leading missions. God impressed on him that He wanted him to do a piece of work that he had been trying to evade. Brown knew what the Lord meant.

His inner struggle continued until February 1921, just one month before the mission was due to start. He nearly resigned from the pastorate because of his unresolved struggle, but he finally acknowledged that God wanted him to do mission work. By the time he set out for Lowestoft the following month, he was ready to be used for every good work (2 Timothy 2:21). Besides those challenges, he was struck down by flu both before and after his arrival at Lowestoft.

In one sense, Lowestoft in 1921 was a typical town on the North Sea coast. However, it had seen revival before. The *land fit for heroes to live in* was going through a depression generally. This is an expression from a speech by the Prime Minister Lloyd George, when he had promised jobs and homes in the UK for ex-servicemen after World War I. In addition to the wider difficulties caused by the depression, Lowestoft had been bombarded by German warships in April 1916. That was just five years previously, and the experience of that had been traumatic.

The mission organisers, Hugh Ferguson and his fellow deacons, were also being tested. Although the church had reached a crescendo of prayer in early 1921, the organisers were concerned whether they could muster an audience for a whole week of meetings.

The mission began well. By the Wednesday evening meeting, there was a 'cloudburst' of people coming forward to the 'inquiry room', and it was estimated that 60-70 people of all ages 'passed from death to life'. There was more great fruitfulness when the meeting was held at the larger Fishermen's Bethel on the Thursday evening, and at the Baptist Church on the Friday evening.

For the following week, they widened the influence of the meetings by holding afternoon Bible studies at Christ Church, an Anglican church. Afternoon meetings at Christ Church and evening meetings at London Road Baptist Church went on from one week to the next.

In the month of mission leading up to Easter, over 500 people were converted. The mission's success led to Douglas Brown making other evangelistic visits to other towns and cities in East Anglia, including Ipswich, Yarmouth, Norwich and Cambridge.

Open-air work was done in Lowestoft in the autumn by a Scottish evangelist called Jock Troup, who was a Salvationist and a *cooper* (barrel maker). He had come from Wick in Scotland to work in the fish-curing yards at Yarmouth. He attracted many to his open-air meetings who had not been impacted by the mission in the spring. His northern Scots accent no doubt helped to draw in many from among the annual working teams and fishing vessels there from North-East Scotland. Hundreds of people were converted.

Separate from that, a travelling event called the Charabanc Crusade took place that summer across many towns and villages in East Anglia, led by the Salvation Army Captains Albert Osborn and Gordon Simpson. There were hundreds of conversions: 106 were recorded in Norwich alone. It is evident that God was working in a multi-faceted way in East Anglia in 1921.

Back home from the fishing season, the Scottish fishermen and their women colleagues went around everywhere in the towns and villages of North-East Scotland preaching the Lord Jesus. Wick and Peterhead were among the towns most greatly impacted, and nearly all the denominations were revived. Salvationists there estimated that thousands were converted in that time of revival in North-East Scotland.[16]

The Lewis Revival, 1949-1952

Many Hebridean islanders had seen revivals before, most recently in 1934 and 1939. Duncan Campbell is the most well-known evangelist associated with the Lewis Revival, otherwise called the Hebridean Revival. He firmly insisted that he did not bring revival, because it was already there. For the islanders, the main person of the revival was not Campbell but the Spirit of God.[17]

The human origins of this revival are associated with two Gaelic-speaking sisters called Christine and Peggy Smith. One was 84 and blind, while the other was 82 and suffering from arthritis. They were burdened to pray for revival because the younger generation on the island were not sufficiently taking on the mantle of faith from the older generation. In Barvas, not one young person attended the church. The two women prayed together twice a week, from 10pm to 3am. One was given a vision of the church filled with young people, while the other could not get out of her mind the promise of God in Isaiah 44:3 'For I will pour water upon him that is thirsty, and floods upon the dry ground' (KJV).

Campbell arrived to lead a mission and conducted his first meeting in Barvas, with about 200 people present, on Wednesday 11th December 1949. He spoke twice every evening in that week, first in a church and later in a home meeting. After the last meeting of the week he recorded in his diary that the Lord had shown His power in a gracious way. The people had not accepted being dismissed at the end of the church meetings, so he had gathered the anxious ones beneath the pulpit and led them to Christ there.

By the second week, Campbell had concluded that they were in the middle of a glorious revival. There were anxious souls to deal with in every meeting, and about 70 adults professed conversion. Some home meetings, later called 'night meetings', continued until 3 or 4am.

When Campbell returned in January, revival began to break out in other parishes, such as Ness. Hundreds of people were crowding into meetings, and others were being turned away. There were several messages to preach every day, and people were being saved daily. He grabbed sleep when he could. People came in busloads to meetings (very few had cars in those days). Two other ministers shared the preaching with him, which gave him some more time to sleep.

Two pipers, who should have been playing in a concert and dance in Carloway, were saved at a meeting in late January. Instead of the pipers going, a brave minister from the district where the dance was being held went there at 3am to tell the young people what had happened. The dance leader was at first reluctant to let him in, but finally let him speak. The minister shared from the final three verses of Psalm 50 ('Repent, all of you who forget me...', v 22). The spirit of God fell upon the gathering, and within ten minutes there were men and women crying to God for mercy. The first to be saved was the leader of the concert party.

By 8th March, revival had gripped much of the island. Campbell counted 14 buses and vans bringing people to a morning meeting. Weekend attendances were on the scale of the Bangor Convention that took place in Bangor in north-west Wales.

The crowded meetings and the number of people being saved continued even while Campbell was away in Edinburgh in

April. Once Campbell returned in late April, the mission that he led in Arnol was one of the toughest he experienced. People opposing the revival set up an opposition meeting just 180m from the church where the meetings were being held. Within two weeks, though, all the opposition was dissolved and the whole district was much more open to the Holy Spirit. Some people needing help after the meetings were in such distress that ministry to them took all night.

A weekend conference was held in Barvas in June, where attendance reached 700. The meetings were especially helpful in breaking down denominational prejudice. The main revival lasted through 1951 and into 1952.[17]

Berneray was then a small, separate island of about 500 inhabitants off the larger Isle of Lewis and Harris. It is now joined to it by a causeway. At Easter 1952, Duncan Campbell was in Bangor, sitting at the front of the Bangor Convention. He received a very strong conviction from the Lord that he should go immediately to Berneray. He had never been there before, but with some difficulty he extricated himself from being the final speaker at the Convention and travelled there as fast as possible.

On arrival by ferry the next day he asked a young man he found standing there to direct him to the nearest minister. He replied there were two churches but no minister, so Campbell asked to be directed to the nearest elder. The young man pointed to a house on the hill, saying that an elder lived there. Campbell asked him to climb up and tell him that Mr Campbell had arrived – 'the Mr Campbell from the island of Lewis' if he wondered which Mr. Campbell this was. The young man came back to say that Hector McKennon had been expecting him to arrive today, and he would be staying with

Mr. McKennon's brother. (In other words, Mr McKennon had previously arranged his accommodation). A church meeting was arranged for him to speak that evening at 9pm.

The evening meeting was just an ordinary kind of service, with a congregation of about 80 people present, and no signs of revival. Afterwards, Hector McKennon assured him that God was hovering over them and that He would break through at any minute. As they walked back down to the main road, behind the congregation, McKennon suddenly took his hat off and said, "Stand, Mr. Campbell! God has come! God has come! See what is happening!" People ahead of them were falling to their knees among the heather, and their cries of penitence could be heard. Everyone returned to the church, and the second meeting lasted from 11pm to 4am. The whole community had been suddenly gripped by God, and a consciousness of Him seemed to hover over the atmosphere.

Mrs McKennon said later that her husband had spent the previous day in prayer. 'He was so concerned about the parish, particularly about the state of the young people, growing up in a state of indifference to God and the church.' On the day that Campbell arrived, her husband had gone three times to the door of the barn where he was praying and she had heard him say, "God, I do not know where he is, but you know, and you send him." There was a man who was looking out for revival.[18]

The North Uist Revival, 1957-1958

North Uist is in the Outer Hebrides and had never had a revival before. Four women in their 20s who were from the Faith Mission, namely Mary Peckham, Jean Wilson,

Mary Morrison and Margaret MacIntyre, spent about a year there. They worked steadily around the island of North Uist, from late 1957 to December 1958. There was considerable resistance from some locals because all four of the missioners were women. Much of their time was spent visiting people, building friendships, praying and singing. They were well supported by visits from Duncan Campbell.

Gaelic singing and solos played a large part. They found that revival singing gets to your whole being. The meetings were characterised by a quiet reverence. The preaching was done in the power of the Spirit and was very direct, with a fearless portrayal of human lostness accompanying the presentation of the gospel. No-one was asked to raise a hand or come forward. People wishing to commit themselves to Jesus were invited to come to a prayer meeting after the service.

An important breakthrough moment happened at Lochmaddy. Doors had been closed against the young women by ministerial choice, and they were obliged to stay in a 'poorhouse' even though there were other districts on the island much more eager to receive them. Convinced that God wanted them there, the young women spent two weeks mainly praying. After that they held a meeting to which 40 came, because 'the minister' Duncan Campbell was speaking. 30 of those then went at midnight to the after meeting, seeking the Saviour.

In mid-January 1958, in the parish of Solas, the young women gained permission to hold a meeting in a school there. They were warned by the Headmaster that they would get no joy there. At the service, many people gave their lives to the Lord, including the Headmaster who came inquiring about his soul.

Islanders who had been unmoved by gospel preaching over decades were suddenly convicted and saved. A famous consequence of the revival was that the pubs on the island were emptied. The young women sought the Holy Spirit's guidance and repeatedly knew beforehand who would be saved in the meetings. Mary Peckham commented that they often felt that they were spectators of what God was doing.[19, 20]

Billy Graham's London Crusade at the Harringay Arena

The Evangelical Alliance (EA) in London gained some new staff in the early 1950s who were keen to see revival. This caused them to invite the American missioner Billy Graham to lead a mission at Harringay Arena, London, in 1954. The crusade lasted 12 weeks, and he spoke to capacity crowds. The closing events were held in Wembley Stadium (capacity 120,000) and White City (capacity 65,000). The overall attendance for the crusade was about 2 million, the largest Christian event in UK history.

The press and some clergy were not at all favourable at first, but the papers at least were publishing more positive articles by the end. Graham stopped after 12 weeks because he was tired. The number who had gone forward at the meetings totalled 38,000. It has been distinctive how many of them went on to be lifelong followers of Jesus Christ. This event was probably the closest point to national revival that the UK has been in the past 100 years.

Prayer, preaching, prophecy and writing about revival

This section considers a few of those who championed revival in the twentieth century. Samples of various speeches can be found on YouTube.

Billy Graham is said to have preached the gospel to more people in live events than anyone else in history. He came from the United States to lead several campaigns to the United Kingdom, of which the crusade at Harringay Arena was the most pivotal. He came back for 7 more crusades in the next 35 years. I heard him speak at one of these, which he did with disarming calmness and clarity.

Martyn Lloyd-Jones was a Welshman who became a medical doctor and later a widely respected minister. He is remembered for his Bible expositions and the books derived from his sermons. He was pastor of Westminster Chapel in London for almost 30 years, in succession to Campbell Morgan. He was extremely interested in revival and managed to transfer his longing for it to many others. In 1959, at the centenary of the 1859 revival, he preached on Revival in a 24-part series.[21]

J. Edwin Orr was an Ulsterman who was greatly inspired in the 1930s by the impacts of revivals. He spent the following decades promoting the subject globally, uniting people to pray for it, researching and teaching about it. He did this to an extent that was perhaps unequalled by anyone else in the twentieth century. He made revival history as well as writing about it. For example, the Easter Revivals of 1936 in New Zealand began during his ministry there. Many of the details given in this book have been drawn from his balanced research into primary sources.

Derek Prince was a Fellow in Philosophy at the University of Cambridge in the 1930s. Despite his scepticism, he came to faith in World War II as a result of reading his Bible. He later became a Pentecostal minister. His teaching has made him one of the best known and respected Bible teachers of all time. I once had the pleasure of sitting down with him and his wife Ruth. His prophecy about coming revival (see chapter 9) led him to help prepare Christians for it.[22]

Duncan Campbell was the visiting missioner in the Lewis Revival. He spent many years as an evangelist attached to Faith Mission in Edinburgh. He became a great author and highly respected authority about revival.

Selwyn Hughes created the Bible reading notes *Everyday with Jesus* and later founded CWR (Crusade for World Revival). The name shows how central revival was to him. I heard him speak more than once. One of his books on revival was *Revival: times of refreshing* (1990)[23], in which he looked at past revivals and explored what revival is and isn't. Churches had been asking him how they could prepare themselves for revival.

Iain Murray is a pastor, author and publisher who has long been an outstanding exponent of Puritan and Reformed beliefs and achievements. In *The Puritan Hope: Revival and the interpretation of prophecy*, he elaborates on the hope for revival. Most particularly, the Puritan hope is most focused on a great ingathering of Jews to the Christian faith, which will be followed by a time of worldwide blessing as seen in Romans 11.[24]

David du Plessis was a South-African born Pentecostal minister. Smith Wigglesworth prophesied over him in the 1930s that God would pour out His Spirit in revival over the historic churches and that he (David) would have a very prominent part in it (see also chapter 9 for more of the prophecy). From the 1950s, he set about taking the Pentecostal experience to other denominations, including the Roman Catholic Church. In the process, he gained the nickname 'Mr Pentecost'.[25]

Arthur Wallis was an evangelist and teacher who had a major role in the beginnings of the Charismatic and Restoration Movements in the UK. He visited Duncan Campbell on the Isle of Lewis in 1951, while the revival there was still happening. His book on revival, *In the day of Thy power*[26], inspired many individuals, as well as some entire missionary organisations, to seek a fresh outpouring of the Holy Spirit. He wrote books to help the contemporary church have foundational materials ready for use at a time of revival, most notably *Living God's way*[27]. I heard him speak several times and had the privilege of meeting him.

Colin and Mary Peckham both had a deep interest in revival. Colin was Principal for 17 years of Faith Mission Bible College in Edinburgh. Mary was converted, as a girl, in the Lewis Revival in 1949. She saw revival first-hand on two more occasions during her ministry. They were the closest to being a living embodiment of revival that I have ever met.[28]

The Restoration Movement

The Movement had its origins in the 1960s. Arthur Wallis and others were seeking God about the coming together of three streams: revival, restoration of New Testament Church, and a Pentecostal emphasis (derived from some who had been part of the Apostolic Church). Out of the revival emphasis came numerous prayer groups and his book on revival.

Restoration was explored and developed in three conferences between 1958 and 1962. At the third, those present heard about the outbreak of the Movement in California. The movement believes in the use of the divinely inspired gifts of tongues, prophecy and others.

Wallis also met Bryn Jones at that third conference a young Welsh evangelist called Bryn Jones, who would become a champion of Restoration church.[29] Some of the prominent individuals of that first generation of the Restoration Movement were or are Gerald Coates, Barney Coombs, David Devenish, Martyn Dunsford (who has been a friend and colleague over many years), Roger & Faith Forster, Dave Mansell (for his prophetic ministry) and Terry Virgo.

Wallis admitted later that, while he had been over-cautious about Pentecostal extremes and imbalance, he and others steadily came to value the place of apostolic ministry in the life of New Testament-style church.

The Renewal Movement

Michael Harper, an Anglican clergyman, founded the Fountain Trust in 1964. The Renewal/Charismatic Movement began to have considerable impact in the UK from the 1970s. It developed out of encounters with the Holy Spirit, which led many to seek greater expression of the Spirit in their own church and life. Renewal reached many Protestant denominations as well as the Roman Catholic Church from the late 1960s. Cardinal Suenens described its place as a current of grace. All the latest Popes have been favourable to it, especially Pope Francis.

Only a few of the more senior Evangelicals in the Anglican church, like John Collins, welcomed the charismatic movement in its early stages. I had the pleasure of visiting him, as well as occasionally hearing the widely respected David Watson of York.

A book aptly entitled *Nine o'clock in the morning*[28] by Dennis Bennett was published in the UK in 1972[30]. It was a wake-up call, little less than a bombshell, to many. He had previously been a theologically liberally-inclined minister, and was filled with the Spirit and transformed into a greater likeness of Jesus as a result.

A time of fruitful evangelism and renewal occurred in the University of Cambridge in the early 1970s, especially around a mission to the university led by David MacInnes in February 1974. A succession of atheists came to faith in those years, among whom I would include myself. About 150 became Christians during the mission itself, associated with a great deal of prayer. Attendance at the Christian Union later reached about 800. Besides that era producing many future church leaders, missionaries and other Christian leaders in their field (such as Ken Costa the financier), there arose the Riding Lights Theatre Company, A Rocha (committed to nature conservation as an expression of Christian mission), the Alpha Course and the Marriage Course. My friend Charles Marnham went on to write the original version of the Alpha Course. Nicky Gumbel repositioned it into the outward-facing course which has now been done by millions of people, in a total of 112 languages.[31, 32]

Learning from each other

Meanwhile, more theologically conservative evangelicals in the UK prospered too, enlivened with a deep love of the Bible and with the guidance of mature leaders, extensive literature and conferences. The Keswick Convention continued to play a valuable part in this. John Stott, Rector of All Souls Langham Place in London, became one of the most respected evangelicals worldwide.

Taking the media opportunities

A roll of honour for media opportunities taken should include mention of: the establishment of CLC (Christian Literature Crusade) as an international mission for distributing Christian literature, the Scripture Union's clever blend of Bible resources and holidays to reach children and young people; John Stott's foresight of a greater potential for Christian publishing; the invasion of the high street book market by Lion Publishing (now Lion Hudson Ltd), founded by David and Pat Alexander; and the multiplication of Bible resources through the ideas and ingenuity of Robert F. Hicks; The radio stations UCB (founded 1987) and Premier Christian Radio (1994) established widespread coverage of the nation.

The Toronto Blessing

In January 1994, a move of God began in a church called the Toronto Airport Vineyard church (now called Catch the Fire Church) in Toronto, Ontario in Canada. Many Christian leaders visited it from other cities and countries in the following three years, totalling an estimated 2 million in all. There were tens of thousands of conversions. Many found refreshing, healing of various kinds, prophetic insights and spiritual release.

News from Toronto was widely circulated. Reports included extensive reference to the somewhat bizarre manifestations seen and heard at some meetings, which included some believers roaring like lions and others making animal noises of different kinds. The church was excluded in December 1995 by John Wimber from the Association of Vineyard Churches.

Thousands of UK churches were impacted in some way by the Toronto Blessing, as it became called.[33] Attempts to reproduce back in the UK what had begun in Canada in the Spirit led to strong differences of opinion in some churches. One way of responding to it positively was to treat it as a fresh encouragement to seek God Himself rather than outward manifestations of His presence.

The Pensacola Revival

A more anticipated move of God began in Pensacola, Florida, in June 1995 at Brownsville Assembly of God (now called Brownsville Church). Paul Yongghi Cho, pastor of the world's largest church in Korea, had prophesied two years earlier in Seattle that God would send a revival to America and that it would begin in Pensacola. In response, the church in Brownsville began immediate preparations.

Then, on Father's Day 1995, the missionary-evangelist Steve Hill started to share about the impact of the Holy Spirit that he had received on a recent visit to Holy Trinity Church, Brompton in London. God came down powerfully that day in Pensacola, and in a way that continued for years afterwards. It is estimated that there were 1.7 million visitors and 100,000 conversions in the following two years. As happened from Toronto, this impacted many UK churches.[34]

Wider impacts

Through these different moves of God and the heartfelt prayers of many during the twentieth century, a countrywide and worldwide church was being forged that would be more capable of attracting and retaining people in a widespread revival.

Thought for Reflection

Following the example of Douglas Brown before his mission to Lowestoft back in 1921, it would be good to reflect whether the Lord might see any reservations in our surrender to Him. There is a moment needed to ask this, as worded below, and a longer time needed to wait for an answer in whatever form that might come.

Prayer

Lord, please tell me if You see any reservations in my surrender to You.

9

The twenty-first century and the coronavirus pandemic

There shall be a great revival in the United States and Great Britain.

(Derek Prince)

There has been no national revival in the UK in this century – yet. However, there have been some remarkable works of God in the past twenty years that help to show that neither God nor His people have exactly been resting. A number of these works of God are mentioned here, in order of appearance.

This has so far been a religious century, in that religion – in one form or another – has seldom been out of the news since 9/11 in New York in 2001. This has often been for other than good reasons. This change of emphasis can be seen to have produced a comprehensible and strong, horrified reaction from some atheists who must have previously contented themselves that the events and 'intellectuals' of the previous century had sent all religion into a final tailspin.

Millennium mishaps

Running up to the start of the new Millennium at midnight on New Year's Eve 31st December 1999, it took some years to put the plans and main building (the Millennium Dome) in place for it. It slowly became apparent in the public realm that both the outgoing Conservative Government and the new Labour one (affirming in 2003 that 'we don't do God') had formed some kind of consensus to keep minimal mention of God and Jesus whose birth had shaped the Millennium being celebrated. Instead, the birth of Jesus was relegated to just one sub-section in the Millennium Experience exhibition, despite Christian protests at the time.

There was in contrast much concern, media coverage and expensive work done about the material matter of the so-called 'Millennium bug'. This was about the identified risk that many computers worldwide might trip out at the same moment when all the year settings changed from '99' to '00'. When it came to the arrival of the Millennium, the Millennium bug did not materialise in any significant way whether people had prepared for it or not. There were varying opinions expressed about it, but at least five major Millennium projects in the country went wrong.

1. The 'River of Fire' was a plan to light up the River Thames at midnight on 31st December 1999, but the display was so little visible to most people when it was activated that it was dubbed a flop.

2. The Millennium Wheel, later renamed the London Eye, was formally opened on 31st December by the Prime Minister but, due to technical difficulties, could not be opened to the public until the following March.

3. The Millennium Dome soon got into financial difficulties, because it did not attract enough visitors. The building was closed before the year was out, and was then sold and converted into a sports arena.

4. The Millennium Footbridge over the Thames also became known as the Wobbly Bridge. This nickname was given because the bridge wobbled so alarmingly when people walked on it that it too had to be closed for around two years, for further engineering work.

5. The Millennium Stone project was to move a 3-ton monolith to Stonehenge from Wales, using only ancient methods to reproduce the original journey of some of the bluestones that there are at Stonehenge. However, the stone was accidentally dropped from a raft into the River Severn, where it remains.

This collection of millennial mishaps, not unnoticed at the time, makes you stop and wonder even now. Encouragingly, since the Millennium, the Queen has taken the opportunity in every one of her Christmas messages to refer to her Christian faith.

24-7 Prayer

24-7 Prayer is a non-stop prayer meeting, a mission and a movement for justice that began in 1999 on the south coast of England, founded by Pete Greig. After a poem from a prayer meeting there went viral, the movement rapidly caught the attention of many young Christians in the UK and across the world. At the last count, 24-7 had reached 2 million people, more than 10,000 prayer meetings, most denominations and people in more than half of the nations worldwide. It has a specific focus on revival. It continues to produce resources for prayer, in terms of books, online and course material.[1]

Soul Survivor

When Gordon Hickson was leading a group of churches in Watford, Ray McCauley who was a visiting preacher from South Africa foretold in the middle of a sermon that there would be a youth revival in their city. He said it would eclipse what was happening across the nation in youth ministry.

Gordon Hickson, who is another friend of mine, naturally assumed that this would happen through the youth ministry in their church. However, a few weeks after that a young Anglican called Mike Pilavachi contacted him, saying that there were only a dozen teenagers in his group but they had a passion to start a youth movement. Hickson quickly realised this was what God had told him about in advance and that his role was not to control it but to pray and to be like a spiritual midwife to it.

The church in Watford let Mike Pilavachi's group use the lounge of a large hostel which they had recently opened. This passionate group of teenagers included some promising songwriters, like Matt Redman and Martin Layzell. The group soon doubled in size, and by that summer it had grown so much that it was allowed to use the church building for its summer gathering. By the next summer (1993) the organisation was large enough to hold the first Soul Survivor Camp at Shepton Mallet.

The camps developed into an attendance of thousands, and at their peak were touching about 35,000 youth every summer. 15,000 young people were converted between 2009 and 2019. As a ministry, Soul Survivor has greatly enhanced youth ministry in the UK and in some other nations too. The Anglican church and some other denominations received the renewing effect of a new, eager generation of young people who joined them.[2] Soul Survivor's large-scale summer events ended in 2019, but the organisation continues to resource the wider church.[3]

The largest annual summer Christian youth event left running in the UK is Newday, which is held near Norwich in Norfolk. Apart from interruptions caused by the pandemic, it too is annually pointing thousands of teenagers to Jesus.[4]

Christians Against Poverty as a move of God to help the very poor

Christians Against Poverty (CAP) is an award-winning Christian charitable company that was founded by John Kirkby in 1996. It has branches across the UK and is also based in a few other countries. It offers a free debt-counselling service for people in financial difficulty. High levels of debt can destroy every good aspect of a person's life, even to the point where some who are in severe debt feel so troubled by their creditors that they do not dare even to get out of bed or open the door to anyone. The charity provides help to plan a pathway out of debt as well as giving immediate assistance with food and other basic necessities. Going debt free is a remarkable experience of release for the person concerned.

It is made clear from the outset to any potential client that CAP is a Christian charity. It helps to signpost people into a better life that can be found in Christ and to introduce them to a caring community of new friends who are associated with a local church. Clients can take the help with their debt problems without accepting any of the Christian opportunities being offered to them. The essential requirement is simply that the client is ready to keep co-operating with the debt-rescue plan that has been agreed with them.

Thousands of the most indebted people in the nation have been helped by this charity, with many going debt free and a large number also responding to Christ. Over 20,000 adults and children were given help by CAP in 2019. Over 2,000 households went debt free in that year, while many others were helped along the journey. The work of CAP has become an ongoing move of God in the nation among the very poor.[5]

The Food Banks movement

Food Banks provide emergency food and additional support to people in crisis. Referrals to a local Food Bank, or an equivalent organisation, are made through a number of statutory and charitable organisations. The supplies are usually donated by supermarkets, wholesalers and other sellers, as well as by members of the public. Much of the work is done by volunteers, as the intention is to turn donations of money into actual aid.

The Trussell Trust is a charity founded on Christian principles which supports a network of 1,200 foodbanks across the country. It was founded in 1997 by Carol and Paddy Henderson. They had become more widely known for their work helping children who were reduced to sleeping rough at the Central Railway Station in Bulgaria. One day, Paddy had a phone call from a mother living in (rather nearer) Salisbury, who told him that her children were going to bed hungry. She asked him what he was going to do about it.[6]

There are also many other food banks, or equivalent organisations, that are part of other charities. The wider network of foodbanks, which has helped to permeate the nation with the practical love of Jesus, has caught the imagination of many of the general public as well as various politicians and journalists. Some people have also come to faith through their new connection with a church. The movement in turn helped to inspire the creation of other (secular) foodbanks during the 2020 lockdown, offering help in connection with community hubs set up by local authorities.

Street Pastors

Street Pastors were pioneered by Les Isaac and first began on the streets of Brixton in 2003. The presence of their teams in city centres at the weekends and other public places has helped to strengthen the night-time economy of communities and to make the streets safer for ordinary people. Some teams operate in the daytime in parks, schools and colleges.

These teams have helped many distressed, homeless and even unconscious people, as well as helping to change the atmosphere of places where it can be risky to be out alone and vulnerable. Volunteers can demonstrate the kingdom of God out on the street, in a powerful and holistic way. Opportunities happen all the time for them to share their faith when asked.

New volunteers undergo 45 hours of training before they go out, equipped with first aid and disarming gifts such as lollipops. A back-up team of prayer supporters pray while their team is out on the streets.

Over 300 towns and cities now have a team, served by over 20,000 volunteers in one role or another who are largely recruited from local Trinitarian-believing churches (who therefore believe in the Holy Spirit). Street Pastors also operate in a number of other countries, mostly English-speaking.

Response Pastors were started in 2014. They are Street Pastors who have had additional training to help them support people affected by a disaster, crisis or emergency. Over 700 of them have been trained so far. Some Response Pastors have had extra training to support disasters management such as the aftermath of the Grenfell Tower fire.[7]

The work of Street Pastors has involved close partnerships with the police and local authorities. This selfless, Christ-like work has spread across the nation and has helped to change the perception of Christians countrywide – and most notably in Parliament. They are even been included in the National Curriculum for Religious Studies. Their 'good Samaritan' work has brought the love of Jesus to many individual people at a difficult moment in their lives.

Coleraine and the founding of Healing on the Streets

Coleraine was the place of some of the most amazing scenes in Ireland during the 1859 Revival. In 1999, a small Vineyard church was planted there by Alan and Kathryn Scott, and they were soon afterwards joined by Mark Marx, a healing evangelist.

It was Alan's visionary initiative to start praying for people on the streets. Once on the street, Mark's experience of town centre-based evangelism and healing ministry quickly turned him into the leading team member there. An Asian woman was healed of arthritis. During outings after that, others were healed from bad backs, broken bones and arthritic conditions.

News of the healings led to Mark being invited by Jamie Watters of the Glasgow Vineyard (church) to lead a healing weekend. During that weekend, a young geologist had a remarkable healing of a shortened leg. A vocal atheist student from her university was converted on seeing this happen before her eyes, and there were over 50 healings that weekend. The church continued to see healings beyond that weekend, as they went out on the streets to pray for people.

Jamie encouraged Mark to turn what he had been teaching about healing into a training format. Writing a training manual for this did not come easily, but finally Mark was able to type out the broad structure of Healing on the Streets (HOTS). An essential element of the concept was to carry God's presence onto the streets and to release God's kingdom with authority there. The ministry had the added benefit of bringing Christians together from different denominations, the importance of which for local revival has been seen repeatedly in this book.

Jamie was asked to lead a healing workshop at the Vineyard National Leaders Conference in Bournemouth (2005), and he asked Mark to join him. Mark had a remarkable encounter with God while at the conference, which radically helped to shape his understanding of what was happening with his ministry. After teaching the theory, they went out onto the pavements of Bournemouth with a banner that simply read 'Healing', and they set out some chairs in a row. A rowdy gang of youths were soon calmed down, many people were healed of back aches and a woman with a severe body rash was instantly healed.

Many Vineyard churches became more outward focused after that conference. In Coleraine, Alan Scott was increasingly convinced that God was doing more beyond the church than in it.[8] With this kind of thinking in view, he said to Mark that it was time to start going after the lost, and they agreed to begin going out weekly. They bought six sturdy wooden chairs, a tall banner and a portable PA. They launched their own HOTS in the market place at Easter 2005. Many of the original team had never seen the sick healed before. They saw not only that happening but lives transformed, people led to faith in Jesus Christ and the power of God released into hurting lives.

They learned to kneel publicly in prayer before the start of a session. They remained kneeling until God's presence came among them, or they finally went home. By the fourth week, a local newspaper carried the headline 'Miracles on our Streets' and featured a photo of Mark holding a walking stick.

The walking stick had been given to Mark by a very grateful 78-year-old veteran who had thought his marching ability was over. A complete boy's football team turned up one day in their football strip. One of them had previously seen two friends healed there. Too many of their players were injured for the team to be able play that day, but they went away healed and the team played their scheduled match. A man called John came along for a whole year, just to watch each week until an unlikely turn of events led him to give himself to the Lord. From all these simple beginnings, a nationwide movement was started, that would impact other nations too in a similar way.[9]

The market place work and the healings in Coleraine continue to this day. Christians in the community became so numerous and bold that it was difficult at times not to be impacted there in some way by the good news of Jesus Christ.

Recent and current champions of revival

The subject of revival continues to have several Christian writers' attention. This section gives a signposting guide to some printed texts of the last 25 years on the subject of revival when seen as a whole, rather than about specific revivals or parts of the United Kingdom.

Terry Virgo's strong interest in revival goes back to hearing the preaching series on revival by Dr. Martyn Lloyd-Jones in 1959. He continues to write articles on revival. Among his many books he has, relevant to this book's title, written

The tide is turning (2006)[10]. I have had the privilege of travelling to see him, to talk expressly about revival.

Nicky Gumbel wrote *The heart of revival* (1997)[11], which explains what revival might mean and how we can prepare for it.

Michael Green wrote *When God breaks in: Revival can happen again* (2015)[12], which includes 'a snapshot of different times of renewal in the history of the British church'. As the title suggests, he encourages the belief that revival can happen again.

Brian Edwards has recently republished *Revival: A people saturated with God* (2019)[13] and *Praying for revival* (2019)[14]. The former book considers some common factors in God's work of revival over many centuries while addressing some human errors and excesses relating to it. His other books include some vivid biographical writing about William Tyndale.[15]

Tony Cauchi is a friend of mine who built up the largest known collection of revival literature in the UK, much of which he has made available online through The Revival Library. He is the author of the informative paper *Overview of revivals* (n.d.)[16].

Michael Marcel has extensively explored the places and people of UK revivals for at least 10 years, under the heading of UK Wells. He has produced online recommendations of places to visit and an informative series of over 20 videos about 'Forgotten Heroes' associated with past revivals. He goes on location and talks well to the camera.

Revival publishing

Publishers with an evident interest in, or category given to, revival include the Banner of Truth Trust, ByFaith Media, CLC Publications, Christian Focus Publications, CWR and DayOne.

The state of the nation in figures

For three years I have been collecting data about the UK and have put these together in an annual summary, which has been increasingly widely circulated. The primary idea of this is that real revival in the nation will surely impact it in some measurable ways. While I cannot predict exactly what those changes will be, this has been an attempt to set up some baseline measures to help verify real revival when it happens.

The latest data, as used here, was collected before the coronavirus pandemic. It is not intended that these figures should be used to hammer audiences with. It is hoped that it will be used for prayer and as a revealing insight of where the UK is now, and has recently been, as a nation.

Most but not all of the figures given here are from reliable online sources, most often the Office of National Statistics (ONS). The reader is cautioned that figures applicable in one year are not likely to be exactly the same in the next year. The providers of data online reserve the right to alter their past figures when they have new information available to them. Population data can look forwards as well as back.

While data itself can be usefully factual, its collection is dependent on the employment, skills, possible biases and loyalties of the people collecting it and on the choice of what data is collected. Even at its best, such data tells us much more about the 'what' than about the 'why' of a situation. The latest annual data is often at least one year behind the current date.

Some of the data about the UK is good news. For example, the country has shown a consistently high level of personal giving, ranking it recently the 7th highest on the World Giving Index[17]. Its influence is seen in the fact that out of the 6 countries that are ranked as having a higher level of giving than the UK, five of them are English-speaking countries.

This ability to give was well illustrated at the time of the lockdown through the hugely generous giving to NHS charities inspired by 'Captain Tom' (Captain Sir Thomas Moore), and to other charitable work that was backed by some celebrities (e.g. the footballer Marcus Rashford was awarded an MBE in October 2020 for services to vulnerable children). The same warm-hearted appreciation shown by the public was seen in the widely shared initiative that had everyone applauding the NHS weekly on their doorsteps.

The country is also ranked as a relatively 'clean' country as regards corruption. Its recent ranking in the Corruption Perceptions Index of Transparency International placed it 12= in the world in 2019.[18]

Most of the other data mentioned here can be seen as a mixture of good news and bad news from a Christian standpoint, and there is some data that is simply neutral information.

Church attendance and church membership have been in a state of slow decline for some time. This has been largely because of reductions in the membership of the major historical denominations, significantly due to their ageing profile. Immigration has generally helped to boost church attendance and membership figures in the country. The ethnic mix in churches is generally increasing. Church attendance figures in Scotland and Ireland have been falling relatively faster, because there has not been the same level of immigration as in England.

The fastest growing churches are: *Pentecostal* churches (a word used to describe churches that place great emphasis on the spiritual powers of the Holy Spirit, usually evidenced by speaking in tongues); immigrant churches, many of them with denominational affiliations; and so-called *opportunity churches* which characteristically plant new churches where there is a need or opportunity, like Hillsong, Newfrontiers, Pioneer, Salt & Light and Vineyard.[19]

Church numbers The number of churches in the UK has been growing slowly. There were recently over 50,000 churches in total. The fastest growing denomination has been the Redeemed Christian Church of God (RCCG).[20]

Marriage and household composition The number of marriages per year (*c.* 300,000 per year in the UK) has been increasing slowly. While the number of marriages in religious ceremonies has continued to decline, the divorce rate is at its lowest for a long time. The low level of divorce is not because fewer are getting married in the first place. It seems that people are thinking more carefully before they get married.

In terms of household composition, there are over 8 million people living alone and nearly 3 million lone-parent families, which leaves a considerable part of the adult population coping, or struggling to cope, with no other adult in the household.

Birth rate. The overall birth rate has been going down. The falling birth rate, clearly impacted by factors such as the decreased number of conceptions and the increased number of abortions (with all the attendant ethical difficulties), has concerning implications for the future scale and impact of the nation.

Household income is an important index of what people's lives are like. Median (the middle amount of) household income is up on the previous year, but the figures for those living in serious poverty have not improved recently.

Debt. Total personal debt has now reached the enormous amount of £1.67 trillion (2020). The cost of servicing the National Debt is equivalent to another 2% of taxable income that could have been spent on something productive. There are, of course, differing views among politicians on the question of sustaining or increasing the level of the National Debt. This figure will anyway go up considerably as a result of the pandemic.

Crime reduction has been a common theme of past national revivals. In fact, crime figures are very difficult to measure exactly. The reliable measures available show that knife crime has increased by 7% (2019), while the amount of crime in general (including murders) has decreased. There are between 600 and 700 murders (homicides) per year.

Health. The *Infant Mortality Rate* (IMR, the number of deaths of children in their first year of life) has stabilised around 3.8 per thousand live births, which is still about double the rate in countries with the lowest figures (Finland has 2%).

About 34% of children in Year 6 are classified as obese or overweight (2018). While the number of deaths related to alcohol or smoking continue to decrease, the number of suicides and the prescription of anti-depressants have both increased. Drug taking, as well as the number of deaths resulting from it, has increased.

Employment. Where Christians and churches are, work is generally encouraged, as that is part of Christian teaching. 32.71 million people were in work in 2019, with about 20% of the population being economically inactive.

The coronavirus pandemic in spiritual perspective

A few observations can be made about the spiritual impact of the pandemic in the UK, as observed so far.

The pandemic and consequent lockdown introduced a time of national and international trauma. There have been comparable traumatic occasions in UK history as a result of severe outbreaks of plague, cholera, Spanish flu, as well as times of famine, war and civil unrest. These times have on the whole helped to turn people towards God, mainly because such times stir more people to ask the big questions of life.

Consistent with such an expectation, research commissioned by Tearfund (and released in May 2020) indicated that almost a quarter of the adult population had watched or accessed a religious service since lockdown, and this was over a third among 18s-34s.[21]

The pandemic produced an interesting difference of reaction between: those churches that believe they are primarily identified by a building, who appeared to be severely curtailed by the 'churches closed' predicament; and those churches who have always maintained that they are primarily a people, who were challenged to live that out without much mobility among their volunteers.

It seems a pity that church leaders of any persuasion did not succeed more than they did in capturing the imagination and attention of the public during the lockdown. Perhaps that could be put down to the rest of us not praying hard enough for such a great breakthrough to occur. There is no shortage of leadership talent out there.

The nation was relatively united at first against a common and invisible enemy, though the national consensus did not last long at the political level. There have been other differences of angry opinion aired too. This has been expressed publicly to an extent that threatens the cultural norms of tolerance won at the cost of many people's lives during the Reformation (as considered in chapter 1, referring to what was forged with so many losses of life in the Reformation period up to the time of Queen Elizabeth I).

There has been a prolonged *silly season*. This is usually an annual media phenomenon in the UK summertime when there is insufficient content for the news outlets, usually experienced in late July and August. In the process, some news becomes headline news that would probably not be so at other times.

A widely circulated video of the horrific death of George Floyd in Minneapolis USA, when under police control, led to much heart-searching right across the world, mainly about what is like to be black in a white majority country. A radical movement that began in the United States, called Black Lives Matter (BLM), gained considerable traction as a result. Protests since then have highlighted this and other tensions in UK society. It is to be hoped that good will come out of this, especially regarding what it is like to be one of the ethnic minorities in the UK (just as the prominent foreigner Joseph pointed out to his brothers that good had come from evil, in Genesis 50:20).

Among Christians worldwide, it was perceived that many of them gave added time to prayer and to reading the Bible. Many churches and individuals did a great deal of praying. Some Christians without much money became generous towards those in greater need. Many people in the wider population sought God for His mercy and grace.[22]

Prophecies about coming revival

Smith Wigglesworth (in 1936) passed on to his spiritual successor David du Plessis a great prophecy of coming revival that seems only partly fulfilled so far. He said that through the old-time denominations there would come a revival that would eclipse anything they had known previously. It would eclipse the present-day, twentieth century Pentecostal revival, along with the strong opposition it had received from the established church.

This same blessing and message would become acceptable to the churches, who would go on with this experience beyond what the Pentecostals had achieved. The Pentecostal movement would be a light thing compared with what God was going to do through the old churches. There would be tremendous gatherings, unlike anything seen previously, and great leaders would change their attitude and accept not only the message but also the blessing.[23]

Derek Prince (in 1953) said that God had spoken to him about revival when he was living in London. 'There shall be a great revival in the United States and Great Britain.'[24] This prophecy had a major effect in shaping his huge international ministry.

Jean Darnell (in 1967) gave a prophecy during a visit to Britain. She had seen the United Kingdom in darkness, but she then saw pinpoints of light that turned out to be fires breaking out from north to south. As these God-lit fires were joined together, they burned brighter. As she continued to pray she saw rivers of fire flowing from north to south; from Scotland, Ireland and Wales into England. Some of the streams crossed into mainland Europe. These fires consisted of people who had been made intensely hungry for the Word of God [referring to the Bible] and for New Testament Christianity. These people would come together and pray. New groups would be formed for prayer and Bible study. She envisaged two moves of God: (1) a renewal of Christian faith and fullness of the Holy Spirit in the church; (2) A national awakening, throughout the land, which would move into every level of the nation's life. It would be great enough to change the character of the nation and determine the future move of God in Europe. Highly anointed preachers would be raised up.

There would also be 'communicators' produced as the rivers of fire moved, who would address the nation through arts, journalism, the radio and television. Actors, singers, teachers and other powerful communicators (with an anointing to work through the media) would work with His army (the younger generation) to reach the hearts of people in continental Europe. People with special anointing would be sent out from the islands of Britain to other nations. The communicators would meet people of similar quality in mainland Europe, who together would release God's work that would result in a spiritual awakening in Europe.[25]

Thought for Reflection

The prophecy given by Jean Darnell can be read partly as a call to prepare. How would it be possible for us to encourage others, or even be involved ourselves, in preparing people deliberately for roles as anointed communicators in each of the main sections of society?

Prayer

Lord, please turn these prophecies into reality in our day.

10

What should I be doing?

Wake up, and strengthen the things that remain.

(Revelation 3:2)

The previous chapters have described the main revivals and other main moves of God that have brought the UK to where it is now from a spiritual point of view. The question is now, What can we do about it? If it happens that you have turned to this chapter first, please read the other chapters before this one.

I hope that reading this book has helped to dispel the idea that another revival could be rather cosy, happy or comfortable. It can be glorious, but it is also demanding, unpredictable, messy, and potentially risky and dangerous for many involved. Some of the toughest opposition has come from other, well-meaning Christians.

It has been interesting to see how God has returned again and again to the same places, bringing some kind of revival there. This list of such places that have been mentioned repeatedly in this book is in no way inclusive. The places include: Aberdeen, Birmingham, Cambridge, Cambuslang (near Glasgow), Cardigan, Carmarthen, Coleraine, Dublin, Dundee, Edinburgh, Glasgow, Gwenapp Pit (Cornwall), the Hebrides, Hull, Kilsyth (near Glasgow), Kingswood (nr.

Bristol), Leeds, Liverpool, London, Lowestoft, Manchester, Oxford and Sunderland. Wider areas of repeated visitations of God have included Cornwall, Scotland, Ulster and Wales. The reader may like to add other places to this list.

It is also striking how many English *revival churches and ministries* there are, that is they have revival in their name or it is otherwise known to be highly valued by them.

As a consequence of this spiritual heritage spread across the British Isles, there are individuals, churches and Christian organisations in many such places, and beyond, seeking God vigorously for revival.

There is a line of Christian thought, which I suggest we should not belong to, that says that revival is such a sacred and sovereign work of God that we must not interfere with it or try to do anything to bring it about. Yet faith without deeds is no faith at all, and the Bible is full of exhortations to action such as to be prepared, wake up, be alert, be holy, be filled with the Spirit, get running, keep going and be faithful unto death itself. Selwyn Hughes wrote about the concept that there are two rails running through scripture that we need to keep on, 'one is the sovereignty of God and the other is the responsibility of man'.[1] The many stories in this book show that revivals characteristically began but did not continue with people only praying.

I suggest that there are three actions we all need to be taking. It may be that you are doing some or all of them already.

Become a learner and a sharer

You may say you are already a learner and a sharer. If so, are you known for it? John Wesley spent years of seeking and learning before he even became a born-again believer, and he then spent the remaining decades of his life trying to help turn his listeners and followers into learners (the Bible word is 'disciples'). Where he or methodism went, education followed. He exhorted his travelling ministers to study for five hours a day. Other people (well-established religious people usually) may have despised 'those methodists' or people like them since then, but their opinions are not a reliable judge. If Wesley's travelling preachers could realistically manage five hours of study a day, with no electricity to help extend their study hours into the night, what could we reasonably manage as a minimum in our busy lives?

All the learning about the Lord is intended to be a prelude to sharing it. The Dead Sea is an unforgettable picture of the Christian who receives an inflow of daily grace but has no outflow. Where is your outflow for what you are learning, or where could it begin?

Be revived yourself

It is very important to be in a thorough state of readiness for revival and not to ignore the need for preparedness as some kind of consolation prize for those who do not see full-on revival. As we have seen in every chapter, revival begins with the people of God, not with the unsaved community. Without trying to copy any of the details, we can emulate that shared, eager approach we have seen in such very different people as John Wesley, Mary Peckham, Evan Roberts, Selina Countess of Huntingdon, Richard Weaver, Smith Wigglesworth and Hector McKennon. We can bless the church and the world by radiating what we have discovered about God and revival. The process has in a sense already begun because you have been taking the trouble to read this book.

Have you ever come across any Christian you would call a walking revival? If so, what has made them like that? What did they – or do they – say on the matter? If you have not met such a person, there are books about such men and women, both living and from the past. Some of these books are listed in the End Notes.

There will probably be some spiritual clearing out to do. There are hurts and sins found in every generation to repent of and cleanse our hearts from, such as pride (an extra-large issue for any history-conscious people like the British), envy, bitterness, jealousy, resentment, anger, anxiety, unforgiveness, materialism, secularism (which is so often coincident with meddling with occult powers), discontent and bullying.

Then there are the hurts and foibles of the current culture of the United Kingdom, which are reinforced almost daily by the world we live in. These include: victim mentality, entitlement, negative criticism, judgementalism, blaming others, self-pity, divisiveness, resistance to authority, confusion of many kinds, a level of casualness that leads to missed opportunities, the kind of self-centred identity that pits one part of the country or community against another, misplaced humour, sexualisation of life as a whole (worst of all affecting children), and lack of purpose and self-worth.

There isn't room in the Spirit-filled life for any of these. This will need some prayer, and maybe some outside help too. People of other cultures or nationalities may like to compile a list that is more customised for their own culture.

Clearing out then needs to be followed by yet more infilling of the Holy Spirit. Jesus made it very clear that we should pray for the Holy Spirit. If we ask God for the Holy Spirit, it is only Him we will receive (Luke 11:9-13). It is then our responsibility to go on being filled with the Spirit (Ephesians 5:18).

You need to ensure you have your own life in order. Revival, as and when it comes, will consume your time and energy while it lasts. There will not be much time then to set other things in order, gain more qualifications, start a new training or do that big DIY project. I was encouraged from my twenties to 'have a light hand on the work' of whatever one is doing, though that has not stopped my involvement in some lengthy projects.

There are relationships to get in order. If you have realised you are out of relationship with anyone as you read this, now is the time to try and get it mended. It's not the other person's responsibility to do that, it's yours – until you have tried your hardest.

It is more than likely there are broken relationships in your wider family. These are, to some extent at least, your responsibility too because you are the one with the light of God to help show the way out of the darkness. What can you do to help bring these disunited relations together? You may be appreciated for attempting it, and you may not. Your intentions may be misunderstood. However, God loves unity. He hates broken relationships anywhere in your family, as disunity produces many bad fruits.

Your own family is a picture of the church. Are you in harmony and unity with everyone in your church, as far as your know? Are there any apologies to be made? Is there forgiveness to be sought or given, including towards yourself? Is there any reparation to be made? The more active your church is, the more likely it is that there are some hurting relationships to be mended.

Are you in unity with believers who are not in your church? If you do not know any of them, and if you do not spend time with any of them, you have certainly not yet reached a state of unity with them. God wants His people united, in some measure at least. Disunity keeps people permanently in lockdown in some ways, while unity can release untold blessing.

We need to turn from a *Christ-crucifying attitude*, the attitude that can be described as driving the nails all the harder into the hands of Jesus on the cross, to a Christ-receiving attitude. We need to turn from paying little attention to sin to grasping the enormity of its destructive power and to turn consciously from it. Sin is a killer (Rom. 6:23). 1 Corinthians 6:9 begins with the question 'Don't you realize that those who do wrong will not inherit the kingdom of God?'

Sin is a subject to be well understood, not quietly ignored. Literally, it means to miss the mark. Translators into English chose the English word 'sin' that was used for an arrow falling short of its target.

It is in the nature of sin to bring down the wrath and judgement of God and is serious enough to have cost Jesus' life on the cross to deal with it. The cross of Christ takes on a new and precious meaning in every revival.[1] There is no space for compromises with sin. Sadly, if it is at all true that the country is overdue for revival, it is even more overdue to receive God's judgement for having squandered so much of its spiritual heritage.

We need to seek out and practise what it means to be *holy*, taken here to mean living and being active in a Jesus-like manner in this world while being at the same time separated to God. We have seen this was a major impulse in the wake of the 1859 Revival: it set many Christians seeking holiness for decades afterwards. We need to seek the Holy Spirit, and all the help that He can bring us. We must avoid *quenching* Him (as in putting out a fire, see 1 Thessalonians 5:19). His work on our character is needed even more than the gifts He can bring us, as the times of testing described in this book have repeatedly demonstrated.

We need to put on, and keep on, our spiritual armour (Ephesians 6:10-20). The people inside the armour (that's us) need to become seasoned warriors for God, not just soldiers who know how to go on parade or how to ride around looking cool like a lone cowboy.

Evan Roberts seemed to know plenty about the Holy Spirit but not so much about the spiritual battle he and others had joined when revival came.

The psalmist prayed 'Revive me according to your word' (Psalm 119:25, NASV). The scriptures are the best possible place for a young person to confirm and establish a lifetime relationship with God: 'How can a young man keep his way pure? By keeping it according to Your word' (Psalm 119:9). The same psalmist loved God's word: it was sweet to taste, sweeter even than honey (Psalm 119:103). Those who loved the scriptures in past revivals the most seem, along with their spiritual descendants, to have lasted the longest.

The one who is truly revived will be unable to keep silent about revival and the great need for it. In the midst of real revival times in 1905, the great Bible teacher Campbell Morgan in London wrote with powerful immediacy in a booklet entitled *The revival: Its power and source*. Chapter 6 'What ought I to do?' brings home graphically that revival begins and continues with the church being awake and active. He explains that there is the need to 'clutch the boon before the moment has passed'. The chapter begins as follows:

> **SPREAD THE GOOD NEWS, and spread it now!**
>
> **If you can do nothing else, send copies of this pamphlet to any relative, friend or other person whom you think may become interested in the subject. Speak to people about it. Write to your friends about it.**
>
> **If you belong to a church, try to get the members interested in the revival.**
>
> **If you are a minister, preach about it, and ask your people to hold prayer-meetings on the subject.**[2]

Become an intercessor for the nation

Every revival's beginning has had the hallmarks of prayer on it. Selwyn Hughes, writing on where revival begins, urged his readers to 'Pray more – in private and in the public prayer meeting.'[1]

Intercession is a specialist form of prayer and is not for the fainthearted. Intercession even at a human level means using your influence with someone in authority to forgive or save somebody else. In prayer, it also involves understanding and grasping God's will and then holding on to it. There is in it a sense of insistence and *importunity* (pressing with repeated requests). Some intercessory prayer is answered rapidly, but a hoped-for answer can take years.

Much of the best intercessory prayer is done alone and unknown. You will hardly ever get much recognition for it, nor should you need it, because most people do not either know or understand what you are doing. However, when there is a prayer meeting arranged, you can be in the starting blocks before it even begins.

'You might be asking, "How long should I pray alone for?" Jesus was disappointed that His young disciples in the Garden of Gethsemane had not lasted one hour at a time of great need, so an hour is a good unit to measure with (Matthew 26:40). Pointless repetition of prayers lasting an hour or more is not the idea.

The state of the United Kingdom cries out for revival. Over 60 years ago, Dr. Martyn Lloyd-Jones called it an urgent and appalling need. Without revival he saw no hope at all for the western world.[3] The UK has moved away from Christian teaching in more ways since then, most notably by its setting aside the sanctity of human life from conception (e.g. compared with the scale and breadth of God's working in the unborn child, as described in Psalm 139). The country is closer now to the seemingly hopeless spiritual state of the known world in New Testament times, yet the gospel broke through even then.

This book has shown repeatedly that the diminished state of the nation has actually been primarily affected by the diminished state of the church and the responses of its leaders and people. Christians and churches have much to repent about regarding ourselves, before getting started on repenting for where the country has got to.

The scriptures give many passages that can be used as a basis for prayers of repentance on behalf of the nation. The scriptures are the place where God began to soften the hearts of people in the British Isles prior to the Reformation, and they still have enormous power. One of the best passages to pray through is Daniel 9:1-19. It can be seen there that Daniel had realised that the 70-year exile of the people of God was coming to an end and that it was the right time to repent thoroughly for all the reasons that had caused their exile.

The Bible writers are amazingly frank with God at times. Two of them even felt the need to urge God to wake up (Psalm 35:23, 44:23)! We need to be frank with Him too, in a reverent way. We need to reinstate the biblical little word, and its reverent meaning, "Oh", into our prayers and sharing. It is that beautiful revival word that the great actor David Garrick most noticed when he heard it from the lips of George Whitefield (as noted in chapter 2).

The enormity of the task involved in praying for the country as a whole (not just your part of it) has hopefully begun to strike you. It must have seemed like that in the past too, for instance when the Clapham Sect were praying about the dire need to end the Slave Trade. God's judgement on the nation was greatly overdue as they saw delay follow delay. Happily, God can make a way where there is no way (Psalm 85:13). As recent aids for this, there is Brian Edwards' recent book on *Praying for Revival*,[4] and Mike Betts in Lowestoft has given many valuable tips for corporate prayer in *The Prayers of Many*.[5]

It is apparent that the scale of God's work in revival means far more than Him doing something extra in our kind of church, though that is quite possibly where collective prayer for revival can begin. It is one of the first intimations of revival that God sets His people 'a-praying'. The stories given in this book have mentioned some of the times when the floods of God's work overflowed the accustomed barriers between denominations and other Christian groupings. Their leaders or volunteers started up what might now be called UPMs (united prayer meetings), and then regularly circulated between them to produce a packed-out auditorium in each others' churches or in public meeting places. As the flow of revival increased among them, these UPMs might be happening somewhere every night.

Please join the army of those already praying daily in some detail for the nation and its leaders. The challenges that people are grappling with in the nation, however well or badly, can become daily material for prayers.

Travelling onwards with God

Although it was not an express purpose of its narrative, this book has helped to show how various new denominations came into being, as some people in established denominations failed to recognise and embrace the move of God happening in front of their eyes. The pattern kept being repeated where the guardians of the old ways drove out, sometimes in very unkind ways, the eager ones who were trying – however clumsily – to put 'new wine into old wineskins'. The challenge is, therefore, to stay as active in our life with God as fresh wineskins, so that we can all hear and recognise it when God is doing a new thing around us. This means not just being ready for change in the distant future but looking out for it now and welcoming, in a thoroughly discerning way, the new things that God is doing.

Thought for Reflection

But don't just listen to God's word. You must do what it says. (James 1:22a)

For Prayer

Lord, please help me to understand, remember and do wholeheartedly what Your word says.

End Notes

Introduction

1 W.E. Sangster, *Revival: The need and the way* (The Epworth Press, 1957).
2 William Blair & Bruce Hunt, *The Korean Pentecost and the sufferings which followed* (The Banner of Truth Trust, 1977).
3 Martyn Lloyd-Jones, *Revival*. Wheaton (Crossway, 1987).
4 Mel Tari & Cliff Dudley, *Like a mighty wind* (New Leaf Publishing, 1997).
5 Rick Joyner, *The world on fire: The Welsh revival and its lessons for our time* (MorningStar Publications, 2013).
6 Michael Green, *When God breaks in: Revival can happen again* (Hodder & Stoughton, 2014).

Chapter 1
The Reformation as a revival and its Puritan legacy

1 Douglas C. Wood, *The evangelical doctor: John Wycliffe and the Lollards* (Evangelical Press, 1984).
2 Merle D'Aubigné, *History of the Reformation in the time of Calvin*. First published in 1863 (HardPress Publishing, n.d.). The abbreviation 'n.d.' means no date of publication was given.
3 Andy Johnston, *Convinced by scripture: The life of Martin Luther* (10 Publishing, 2017)
4 William A. Clebsch, *England's earliest Protestants 1520-1535* (Yale University Press, 1964), 42, 46.
5 Michael Reeves, *The unquenchable flame: Discovering the heart of the Reformation* (Inter-Varsity Press, 2009), Chapter 5
6 Iain Murray, *The Puritans and revival Christianity*. First published in 1969. Retrieved from GraceOnlineLibrary.
7 Marcus Loane, *Masters of the English Reformation*. First published in 1954 (Banner of Truth, 2005).

8 Merle D'Aubigné (Edited by S.M. Houghton), *The Reformation in England*, Vols. 1 & 2. From works published in 1866-78 (Banner of Truth, 1963).
9 Elizabeth Whitley, *The plain Mr. Knox* (Christian Focus Publications, 2001).
10 Melvyn Bragg, *The book that brought freedom* (*The Sunday Times*, March 2011).
11 J. Wesley Bready, *England before and after Wesley: The English revival and social reform* (Hodder & Stoughton, 1938).
12 Matthew Henry, *Matthew Henry's commentary on the whole Bible: Complete and unabridged.* First published in 1708-1710 (Hendrickson, 2008).
13 Jim I. Packer, *Puritan Portraits* (Christian Focus Publications, 2012).
14 Richard Owen Roberts (Ed.) (1995). *Scotland saw His glory: A history of revivals in Scotland* (International Awakening Press, 1995).

Chapter 2
The Evangelical Awakening beginning in 1727

1 William Doddridge. The works of Philip Doddridge, Volume 1. First published in 1765. (HardPress Publishing, 2017), 31.
2 Michael Balen, *A very English deceit: The secret history of the South Sea Bubble and the first great financial scandal* (Fourth Estate, 2002).
3 J. Wesley Bready, *England before and after Wesley: The English revival and social reform* (Hodder & Stoughton, 1938), 192.
4 Tom Lennie, *Land of many revivals: Scotland's extraordinary legacy of Christian revivals over four centuries 1527-1857* (Christian Focus Publications, 2015), 147-149
5 Robert Southey, *The life of John Wesley.* First published in 1820 (Rare Books Club, 2012)
6 J. Wesley Bready, *England before and after Wesley: The English revival and social reform*, Chapters 10-15.
7 Arnold A. Dallimore, *A heart set free: The life of Charles Wesley* (Crossway Books 1988).
8 Arnold A. Dallimore, *George Whitefield: The life and times of the great evangelist of the 18th century revival* (Banner of Truth, 1980).
9 Faith Cook, *Selina Countess of Huntingdon* (Banner of Truth, 2001).
10 Faith Cook, *William Grimshaw of Howarth* (Banner of Truth, 1997).

11 J. Wesley Bready, *England before and after Wesley: The English revival and social reform*, 394-395

12 J. Wesley Bready, *England before and after Wesley: The English revival and social reform*, 228-229

Chapter 3
Aftermath of the Evangelical Awakening

1 J. Edwin Orr, *The eager feet: Evangelical awakenings 1790-1830* (Moody Press, 1975), Chapter 2.

2 J. Edwin Orr, *The eager feet: Evangelical awakenings 1790-1830*, Chapter 3.

3 Tom Lennie, *Land of many revivals: Scotland's extraordinary legacy of Christian revivals over four centuries 1527-1857* (Christian Focus Publications, 2015). See the book title.

4 J. Edwin Orr, *The eager feet: Evangelical awakenings 1790-1830*, Chapter 4.

5 J. Edwin Orr, *The eager feet: Evangelical awakenings 1790-1830*, Chapter 5.

6 Kevin Belmonte, *William Wilberforce: A hero of humanity*, 2nd ed. (Zondervan, 2007).

7 J. Wesley Bready, *England before and after Wesley: The English revival and social reform* (Hodder & Stoughton, 1938), Chapter 18.

8 Margaret Bryant, *The Clapham Sect* (The Clapham Society, 2004).

9 J. Edwin Orr, *The eager feet: Evangelical awakenings 1790-1830*, 105.

Chapter 4
Later descendants of the Evangelical Awakening

1 J. Wesley Bready, *England before and after Wesley: The English revival and social reform* (Hodder & Stoughton, 1938).

2 J. Edwin Orr, *The eager feet: Evangelical awakenings 1790-1830* (Moody Press, 1975), Chapter 14.

3 J. Edwin Orr, *The eager feet: Evangelical awakenings 1790-1830*, Chapter 20.

4 Robert Duncan, *Perthshire's Revival Century, 1799-1905* (Oasis Church, Perth, 2016). Retrieved from http://www.oasischurchperth.org.uk/wp-content/uploads/2013/10/Perthshire-Revivals-in-the-Nineteenth-Century.pdf

5 Tom Lennie, *Land of many revivals: Scotland's extraordinary legacy of Christian revivals over four centuries 1527-1857* (Christian Focus Publications, 2015), 329-334.
6 Mathew Backholer, *Revival fires and awakenings: Thirty-six visitations of the Holy Spirit* (6th ed.) (ByFaith Media, 2017), 48.
7 Owen Rattenbury, *Flame of Freedom: The romantic story of the Tolpuddle Martyrs*, 2nd ed. (Owen Rattenbury, 1933).
8 J. Wesley Bready, *Lord Shaftesbury and social-industrial progress* (George Allen & Unwin, 1926).
9 J. Edwin Orr, *The eager feet: Evangelical awakenings 1790-1830*, Chapter 25.

Chapter 5
The 1859 Revival

1 J. Edwin Orr, *The second evangelical awakening in Britain* (Marshall, Morgan & Scott, 1949).
2 Tony Cauchi, *Overview of revivals* (The Revival Library, n.d.).
3 J. Edwin Orr, *The second evangelical awakening in Britain*, Chapter 1.
4 Ibid. (= the same as the reference above), Chapter 2.
5 Ibid., Chapter 4.
6 Robert Duncan, *Perthshire's Revival Century, 1799-1905* (Oasis Church, Perth, 2016). Retrieved from http://www.oasischurchperth.org.uk/wp-content/uploads/2013/10/Perthshire-Revivals-in-the-Nineteenth-Century.pdf
7 J. Edwin Orr, *The second evangelical awakening in Britain*, Chapter 3.
8 Ibid., Chapter 5.
9 Ibid., Chapter 6.
10 Ibid., Chapter 7.
11 Charles G. Finney, *Lectures on revivals of religion*. First published in 1868 (Christian Classics Treasury, n.d.)

Chapter 6
Aftermath of the 1859 Revival

1 J. Edwin Orr, *The second evangelical awakening in Britain* (Marshall, Morgan & Scott, 1949), Chapter 10.
2 Keswick Ministries, *Keswick Convention 2021* (2020). Retrieved from https://keswickministries.org/

3 Charles. H. Spurgeon, *Autobiography 2: The full harvest 1860-1892.* First published 1897-1900 (Banner of Truth, 1973), 193.

4 Charles. H. Spurgeon, *Only a prayer meeting: Forty addresses at Metropolitan Tabernacle and other prayer-meetings.* First published in 1901 (Christian Classics Treasury, 2015).

5 Robert Backhouse (Ed.), *Spurgeon on revival* (Kingsway, 1996).

6 C.H. Spurgeon, *Autobiography 2: The full harvest 1860-1892*, 378.

7 J. Wesley Bready, *Doctor Barnardo: Physician, pioneer, prophet* (George Allen & Unwin, 1932).

8 John Pollock, *The Cambridge Seven: The true story of ordinary men used in no ordinary way* (Christian Focus, 2012).

9 William R. Moody, *The Life of D.L. Moody by his son.* First published in 1900 (Nabu Press, 2013).

10 Tom Lennie, *Scotland ablaze: The twenty-year fire of revival that swept Scotland 1858-79* (Christian Focus, 2018), Chapter 22.

11 The Salvation Army, *Home page* (2020). Retrieved from https://www.salvationarmy.org.uk/

12 Biography online, *William Booth biography* (n.d.). Retrieved from https://www.biographyonline.net/spiritual/william-booth.html

13 Bob Holman, *Keir Hardie: Labour's greatest hero?* (Lion Books, 2010).

Chapter 7
The Welsh Revival of 1904-1905 and beyond

1 Kevin Adams & Emyr Jones, *A pictorial history of revival: The outbreak of the 1904 Welsh awakening* (CWR, 2004).

2 Kevin Adams, *A diary of revival: The outbreak of the 1904 Welsh awakening* (CWR, 2004), 19-21.

3 J. Edwin Orr, *The flaming tongue: The impact of twentieth century revivals* (Moody Press, 1973), Chapter 1.

4 J. Edwin Orr, *The flaming tongue: The impact of twentieth century revivals*, Chapter 2.

5 Ibid., Chapter 3.

6 Olig532, *Here is love vast as the ocean – in Welsh and English* (YouTube, n.d.). Retrieved from https://www.youtube.com/watch?v=KZJmTVdDyLY

7 Selwyn Hughes, *Revival: Times of refreshing* (CWR, 1990), 73.

8 S.B. Shaw, *The great revival in Wales*. First published 1905 (Christian Life Books, 2014), p.76.
9 J. Edwin Orr, *The flaming tongue: The impact of twentieth century revivals*. Chapter 4.
10 Tom Lennie, *Glory in the glen: A history of evangelical revivals in Scotland 1880-1940* (Christian Focus, 2009). p.99.
11 J. Edwin Orr, *The flaming tongue: The impact of twentieth century revivals*. Chapter 5
12 Ibid., Chapters 6-23.

Chapter 8
The rest of the twentieth century

1 Mark A. Noll, *Turning points: Decisive moments in the history of Christianity* (3rd ed.). Baker Academic, 2012), 262-264.
2 Stanley Frodsham, *With signs following: The story of the Latter-Day Pentecostal Revival* (Revival Library Reprints, (n.d.), 66-73.
3 Donald Gee, *The Pentecostal Movement: A short history and an interpretation for British readers* (Lightning Source UK, 2010), 22-23.
4 Monkwearmouth Parish, *All Saints Church Visitor Information* (2019). Retrieved from https://monkwearmouthcofe.com/all-saints
5 David Du Plessis, *A man called Mr. Pentecost* (Logos International, 1977).
6 Donald Gee, *The Pentecostal Movement: A short history and an interpretation for British readers*, 34-35.
7 Rachel Guzman De Vlugt, *Smith Wigglesworth biography* (Inspirational Christians, 2016). Retrieved from https://www.inspirationalchristians.org/evangelists/smith-wigglesworth/
8 J. Edwin Orr, *The flaming tongue: The impact of twentieth century revivals* (Moody Press, 1973), Chapter 24.
9 Stanley Frodsham, *With signs following: The story of the Latter-Day Pentecostal Revival* (Revival Library Reprints, (n.d.). p. 77.
10 J. Edwin Orr, *The flaming tongue: The impact of twentieth century revivals*. Chapter 25.
11 Gavin Wakefield, *Alexander Boddy: Pentecostal Anglican Pioneer* (Paternoster, 2007), pp. 105-106.
12 Donald Gee, *The Pentecostal Movement: A short history and an interpretation for British readers*, Chapter 2.

13 Redeemed Christian Church of God, *Our history* (2020). Retrieved from https://www.rccguk.church/our-history/
14 Elim, *We are Elim* (n.d.). Retrieved from https://www.elim.org.uk/Groups/243050/About_Elim.aspx
15 Assemblies of God, *Home* (2019). Retrieved from https://www.aog.org.uk/
16 Griffin, S.C. (1992). *A forgotten revival: East Anglia and North-East Scotland 1921*. Bromley: DayOne Publications.
17 Colin and Mary Peckham, *Sounds from heaven: The revival on the Isle of Lewis, Scotland, 1949-1952* (Christian Focus Publications, 2004).
18 Duncan Campbell, *The nature of a God-sent revival* (Christlife Publishers, 1993), 12-14
19 Mathew Backholer, *Revival fires and awakenings: Thirty-six visitations of the Holy Spirit* (6th ed.) (ByFaith Media, 2017), 107-109.
20 Richard Duncan, *Revivals in Scotland in the 20th century: The Hebrides and North Uist* (n.d.). Retrieved from http://www.oasischurchperth.org.uk/wp-content/uploads/2013/11/The-Hebrides-Revivals-1949-52-and-1957-58.pdf
21 Martyn Lloyd-Jones, *Revival.* Wheaton (Crossway, 1987).
22 Derek Prince, *The coming revival: Shaping history for a new heavenly reality* (DPM-UK, (2019).
23 Selwyn Hughes, *Revival: Times of refreshing* (CWR, 1990).
24 Iain H. Murray, *The Puritan hope: Revival and interpretation of prophecy* (Banner of Truth, 1971).
25 David Du Plessis, *A man called Mr. Pentecost*, 3
26 Arthur Wallis, *In the day of Thy power* (CLC Publications, 2010).
27 Arthur Wallis, *Living God's way* (Kingsway, 1984).
28 Colin and Mary Peckham, *Sounds from heaven: The revival on the Isle of Lewis, Scotland, 1949-1952* (Christian Focus Publications, 2004).
29 Arthur Wallis, Springs of restoration 1 & 2, *Restoration* (1980, July/Aug & Sept/Oct).
30 Dennis Bennett, *Nine o'clock in the morning.* First published in 1972 (Bridge Logos, 2020).
31 Gordon Hickson, *Harnessed for adventure: True life stories of faith adventures with God* (Heartcry Ministries, 2019), Chapter 4.
32 Alpha International, *You're invited* (n.d.). Retrieved from alpha.org.uk

33 Catch the Fire Church, *About us* (n.d.). Retrieved from ctftoronto.com/about
34 Brownsville Church, *Honoring our past* (n.d.). Retrieved from Brownsville.church/about-us/history

Chapter 9
The twenty-first century and the coronavirus pandemic

1 24-7 Prayer, *It all started by accident* (n.d.). Retrieved from https://www.24-7prayer.com/story#/24-7story/prayer-explosion
2 Gordon Hickson, *Harnessed for adventure: True life stories of faith adventures with God* (Heartcry Ministries, 2019).
3 Soul Survivor, *Home page* (n.d.). Retrieved from soulsurvivor.com
4 Newday (2020). *Future dates.* Retrieved from https://newdaygeneration.org/blog/future-festival-dates
5 Christians Against Poverty, *The CAP story* (n.d.). Retrieved from https://capuk.org/about-us/the-cap-story
6 Trussell Trust, *Our story* (2020). Retrieved from https://www.trusselltrust.org/ about/our-story/
7 Street Pastors, *About us* (2020). Retrieved from https://www.streetpastors.org/about-us-1/
8 Alan Scott, *Scattered servants* (David C Cook, 2018).
9 Mark Marx, *Stepping into the impossible* (River Publishing and Media, 2015).
10 Terry Virgo, *The tide is turning* (New Wine Press, 2006).
11 Nicky Gumbel, *The heart of revival* (Kingsway, 1997)
12 Michael Green, *When God breaks in: Revival can happen again* (Hodder & Stoughton, 2014).
13 Brian Edwards, *A people saturated with God* (Day One Publications, 2019).
14 Brian Edwards, *Praying for revival* (Day One Publications, 2019).
15 Brian Edwards, *God's outlaw: The story of William Tyndale and the English Bible* (Evangelical Press, 1982).
16 Tony Cauchi, *Overview of revivals* (The Revival Library, n.d.).
17 Charities Aid Foundation, *World Giving Index* (10th ed.). Retrieved from https://www.cafonline.org/about-us/publications/2019-publications/caf-world-giving-index-10th-edition#tab1

18 Transparency International, *Corruption Perceptions Index 2019.* Retrieved from https://www.transparency.org/en/cpi

19 Peter Brierley, *Does the church have a future?* (Brierley Consultancy, 2020)

20 Redeemed Christian Church of God, *Our history* (2020). Retrieved from https://www.rccguk.church/our-history/

21 Tearfund, *Many Brits look to faith during lockdown* (May 2020). Retrieved from https://www.tearfund.org/media/press_releases/many_brits_look_to_faith_during_lockdown/

22 CLC International, 2019 world report, *CLC world magazine* (2020).

23 David Du Plessis, *A man called Mr. Pentecost* (Logos International, 1977), 2-3.

24 Derek Prince, *The coming revival: Shaping history for a new heavenly reality* (DPM-UK, (2019), page ix

25 ByFaith Media, *British revival vision: Jean Darnell 1967.* Retrieved from https://www.byfaith.co.uk/paulrevival4.htm

Chapter 10

What should I be doing?

1 Selwyn Hughes, *Revival: Times of refreshing* (CWR, 1990), 85.

2 W.T. Stead & G. Campbell Morgan, *The Welsh revival – I. A narrative of the facts. 2. The revival: Its power and source.* First published 1905 (CrossReach Publications, 2019).

3 Martyn Lloyd-Jones, *Revival.* Wheaton (Crossway, 1987).

4 Brian Edwards, *Praying for revival* (Day One Publications, 2019).

5 Mike Betts, *The prayers of many: Many people, many places, one voice* (Relational Mission, 2019).

Ongoing developments

'Change of the tide' blog

There is the blog 'Change of the Tide' at Wordpress, https://changeofthetide.blog

You can sign up on that website to receive the entries as they are published, by scrolling to the bottom of all the blog entries so far. This website was begun in 2017. It addresses some contemporary issues, where the sound of another Christian voice about current affairs has seemed helpful. The goal of it all is social transformation. Topics typically focus on a policy area or some aspect of public or national life, and are addressed from a positive and non-party viewpoint. Titles already posted include:

☑ Anticipating a change of the tide

☑ Health and the NHS

☑ Education in the UK

☑ A time of social change

KCC blogs

There are also blogs on revival topics for a Christian audience that have been written by the author. They can be found among other entries on the blog page of King's Community Church (Southampton), usually called 'KCC', at https://www.kccsouthampton.org/blog

These blog entries have given the author the opportunity to write with more obviously Christian wording than is appropriate for the wide readership of the Change of the

Tide blogs. They focus a little more expansively on a revival topic than has been suitable for this book. They address some matters that have been raised by other people, or they may concern issues where there are some genuine differences of opinion among evangelical Christians. Titles of this kind already posted are:

- ☑ Is it possible to bring about a revival?
- ☑ Metaphors of revival
- ☑ Thrilling feelings of revival

The wider Christian scene in the UK

The UK church has become much more outward looking than it was, helped especially by church networks and the Cinnamon Network. Regular events have included the Keswick Convention, Spring Harvest, New Wine, Big Church Day Out, CRE (the Christian Resources Exhibition), and Big Church Night Out. Evangelists like J John, Adrian Holloway, Glen Scrivener, Steve Lee and from Through Faith Missions are among those impacting the nation with the gospel. Huge amounts of prayer have been undergirded by organisations like the World Prayer Centre and 24/7. God TV has gone worldwide. International Christian work continues to thrive, both through sending missionary organisations like WEC (World Evangelisation Crusade) and the international student ministry of Friends International.

Revival can move God's work to a new dimension. Each town and city has its own special calling in God's purposes. Come Wind of God, blow upon the United Kingdom!